Donna Kooler's Cross-Stitch Designs

333 Patterns for Ready-to-Stitch Projects

Donna Kooler's Cross-Stitch Designs

333 Patterns for Ready-to-Stitch Projects

Sterling Publishing Co, Inc., New York
A Sterling/Chapelle Book

Kooler Design Studio

President: Donna Kooler
Executive Vice President: Linda Gillum
Vice President: Priscilla Timm

Editor: Priscilla Timm
Contributing Editors: Deanna Hall West, Arlis Johnson
Charters: Deanna Hall West, Lennea LaHammedieu
Designers: Linda Gillum, Barbara Baatz, Sandy Orton,
Jorja Hernandez, Nancy Rossi, Pam Johnson,
Robin Kingsley, Holly DeFount, Donna Yuen
Design Assistants: Sara Angle, Anita Forfang,
Virginia Hanley-Rivett, Marsha Hinkson, Lori Patton,
Char Randolph, Giana Shaw
Proof Readers: Arlis Johnson, Anita Forfang

Photographer: Dianne Woods, Berkeley, California
Photo Stylists: Donna Kooler, Deanna Hall West
Cross-stitch Program: Pattern Maker for Cross stitch
Hobby Ware, Inc.
Indianapolis, IN

Library of Congress Cataloging-in-Publication Data Available

10 9 8 7 6 5 4 3 2 1

A Sterling/Chapelle Book

First paperback edition published in 2001 by
Sterling Publishing Company, Inc.
387 Park Avenue South, New York, NY 10016
© 2000 by Chapelle Ltd.
Distributed in Canada by Sterling Publishing
% Canadian Manda Group, One Atlantic Avenue, Suite 105
Toronto, Ontario, Canada M6K 3E7
Distributed in Great Britain and Europe by Cassell PLC
Wellington House, 125 Strand, London WC2R 0BB, England
Distributed in Australia by Capricorn Link (Australia) Pty Ltd.
P.O. Box 6651, Baulkham Hills, Business Centre, NSW 2153, Australia
Printed in China
All Rights Reserved

Sterling ISBN 0-8069-3796-3 Trade
0-8069-3703-3 Paper

Chapelle Ltd.

Owner: Jo Packham

Editor: Linda Orton

Welcome to Kooler Design Studio's first book of patterns especially designed to be used on premade articles.

These designs were created for when you want the perfect baby gift, a mug for your favorite neighbor, a bookmark for your mother, or a token of friendship for someone special. In this collection you will find the perfect choice which can easily be stitched in a few hours or days and finished without any sewing! Quick and easy–what a boon this is in the fast-paced world where time has become a precious commodity.

With our 333 designs, you can create an endless array of beautiful projects.

Let your imagination run wild and enjoy!

Dedicated to R. Scott Horton for his patience and knowledge.

A special thanks to Adam Original, Charles Craft, Crafter's Pride, Jeanette Crews, MCG Textiles, and Zweigart for their ready-to-stitch products.

If you have any questions or comments, please contact:

Chapelle Ltd., Inc.
P.O. Box 9252
Ogden, UT 84409

Phone: (801) 621-2777
FAX: (801) 621-2788
e-mail: Chapelle@aol.com

Table of Contents

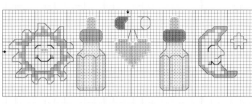

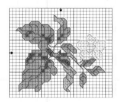

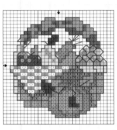

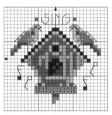
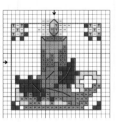

General Instructions

Introduction

333 patterns for ready-to-stitch projects have been included in *Donna Kooler's Cross-Stitch Designs* and in most cases require very minimal or no construction.

Fabric for Cross-stitch

Counted cross-stitch is worked on even-weave fabrics, such as Aida. These fabrics are manufactured primarily for counted-thread embroidery, and are woven with the same number of vertical as horizontal threads per inch.

Because the number of threads in the fabric is equal in each direction, each stitch will be the same size. The number of threads per inch in even-weave fabrics determines the size of a finished design.

Number of Floss Strands

The number of strands used per stitch varies, depending on the fabric used. Generally, the rule to follow for cross-stitching is three strands of floss on Aida 11, two strands on Aida 14, one or two strands on Aida 18 (depending on desired thickness of stitches), and one strand on Hardanger 22.

For backstitching, use one strand on all fabrics. When completing a french knot, use two strands and one wrap on all fabrics, unless otherwise directed.

Finished Design Size

To determine the size of the finished design, divide the stitch count by the number of threads per inch of fabric. When the design is stitched over two threads, divide stitch count by half the threads per inch. For example, if a design with a stitch count of 120 width and 250 length were stitched on a 28-count linen over two threads, use the following formula: 120 (stitch width) divided by 14 (stitches per inch) = 8⅝" and 250 divided by 14 = 17⅞", to determine the finished design size of 8⅝" x 17⅞".

Preparing Fabric

Cut fabric at least 3" larger on all sides than the finished design size to ensure enough space for desired assembly. To prevent fraying, whipstitch or machine-zigzag along the raw edges or apply liquid fray preventive.

Needles for Cross-stitch

Blunt needles should slip easily through the fabric holes without piercing fabric threads. For fabric with 11 or fewer threads per inch, use a tapestry needle size 24; for 14 threads per inch, use a tapestry needle size 24 or 26; for 18 or more threads per inch, use a tapestry needle size 26. Never leave the needle in the design area of the fabric. It may leave rust or a permanent impression on the fabric.

Floss

All numbers and color names on the codes represent the DMC brand of floss. Use 18" lengths of floss. For best coverage, separate the strands and dampen with a wet sponge. Then put together the number of strands required for the fabric used.

Centering Design

Fold the fabric in half horizontally, then vertically. Place a pin in the fold point to mark the center. Locate the center of the design on the graph. To help in centering the designs, arrows are provided at left-center and top-center. Begin stitching all designs at the center point of the graph and fabric.

Securing Floss

Insert needle up from the underside of the fabric at starting point. Hold 1" of thread behind the fabric and stitch over it, securing with the first few stitches. To finish thread, run under four or more stitches on the back of the design. Never knot floss, unless working on clothing.

Another method of securing floss is the waste knot. Knot floss and insert needle down from the right top side of the fabric about 1" from design area. Work several stitches over the thread to secure. Cut off the knot later.

Carrying Floss

To carry floss, weave floss under the previously worked stitches on the back. Do not carry thread across any fabric that is not or will not be stitched. Loose threads, especially dark ones, will show through the fabric.

Cleaning Finished Design

When stitching is finished, soak the fabric in cold water with a mild soap for five to ten minutes. Rinse well and roll in a towel to remove excess water. Do not wring. Place the piece face down on a dry towel and iron on a warm setting until the fabric is dry.

Cross-stitch (XS)

Stitches are done in a row or, if necessary, one at a time in an area.

1. Insert needle up between woven threads at A.

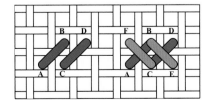

2. Go down at B, the opening diagonally across from A.

3. Come up at C and go down at D, etc.

4. To complete the top stitches creating an "X", come up at E and go down at B, come up at C and go down at F, etc. All top stitches should lie in the same direction.

Backstitch (BS)

1. Insert needle up between woven threads at A.

2. Go down at B, one opening to the right.

3. Come up at C.

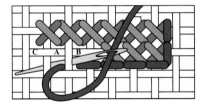

4. Go down at A, one opening to the right.

French Knot (FK)

1. Insert needle up between woven threads at A, using one strand of embroidery floss.

2. Loosely wrap floss once around needle.

3. Go down at B, the opening across from A. Pull floss taut as needle is pushed down through fabric.

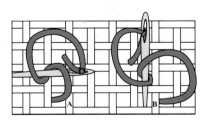

4. Carry floss across back of work between knots.

Designs for Baby

Pink Gingham hooded bath towel (as shown on page 9)
Stitch Count: 116 width x 78 length
left

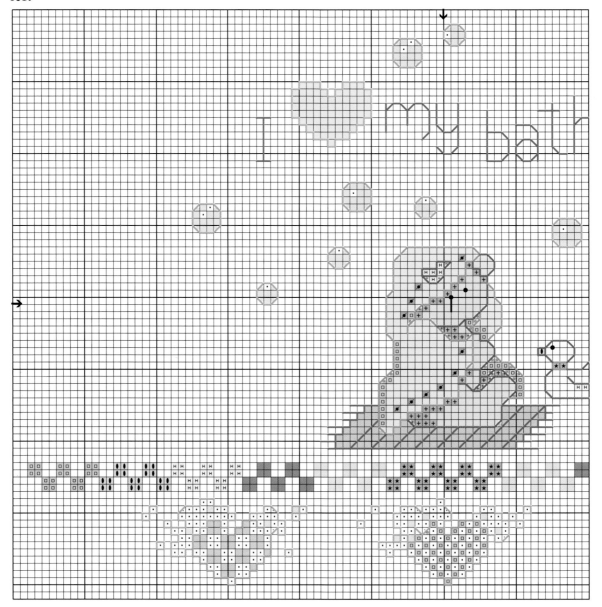

Flower mitten
(as shown on page 9)
Stitch Count: 13 width x 19 length

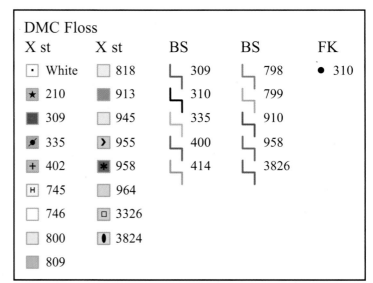

DMC Floss				
X st	X st	BS	BS	FK
· White	818	309	798	● 310
★ 210	913	310	799	
309	945	335	910	
335	› 955	400	958	
+ 402	* 958	414	3826	
H 745	964			
746	□ 3326			
800	3824			
809				

right

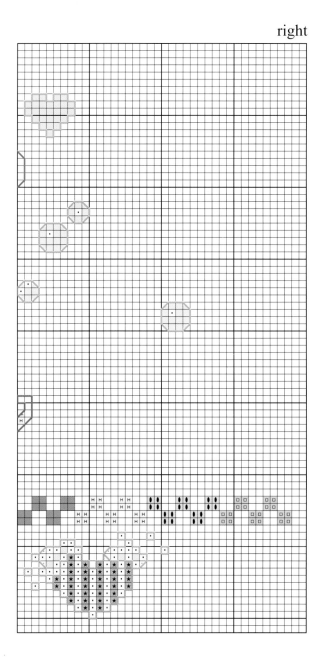

Vine Flower bonnet (right side)
(as shown on page 9)
Stitch Count: 21 width x 32 length

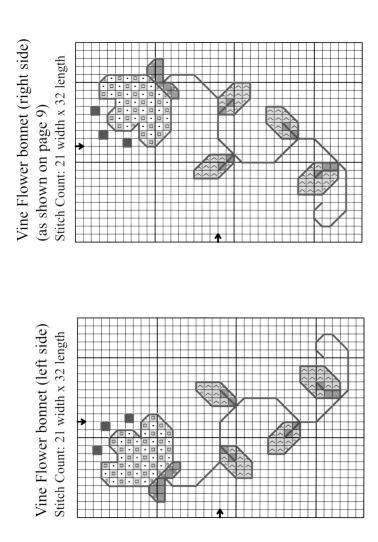

Vine Flower bonnet (left side)
Stitch Count: 21 width x 32 length

Bear mitten
(as shown on page 9)
Stitch Count: 13 width x 15 length

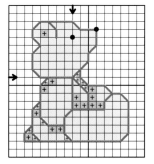

Heart bootie
(as shown on page 8)
Stitch Count: 11 width x 13 length

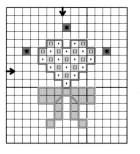

Bear bootie
(as shown on page 8)
Stitch Count: 13 width x 13 length

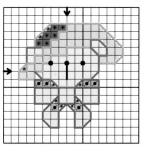

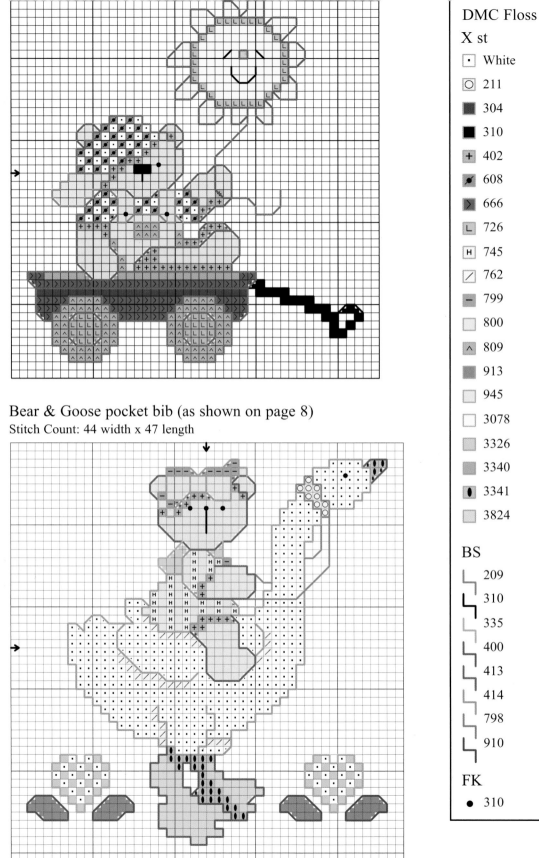

Bear & Goose pocket bib (as shown on page 8)
Stitch Count: 44 width x 47 length

DMC Floss

X st

·	White
◯	211
▨	304
■	310
+	402
✦	608
▶	666
L	726
H	745
/	762
–	799
▢	800
∧	809
▨	913
▨	945
▢	3078
▨	3326
▨	3340
◗	3341
▨	3824

BS

⌐	209
⌐	310
⌐	335
⌐	400
⌐	413
⌐	414
⌐	798
⌐	910

FK

●	310

Bear cup (as shown on page 8)
Stitch Count: 78 width x 26 length

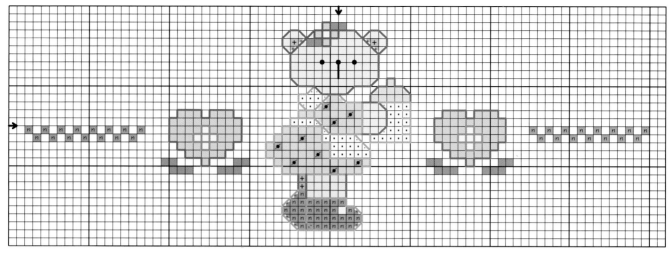

I'm a Star bootie (as shown on page 17)
Stitch Count: 18 width x 13 length

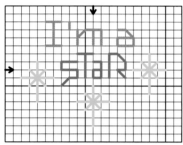

Bear & Flower round bib (as shown on page 9)
Stitch Count: 35 width x 40 length

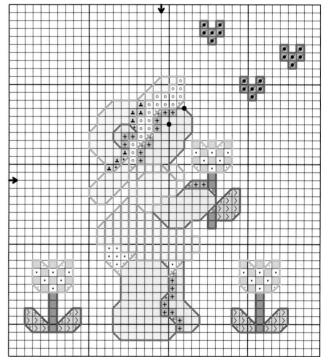

A Star is Born bootie (as shown on page 17)
Stitch Count: 22 width x 17 length

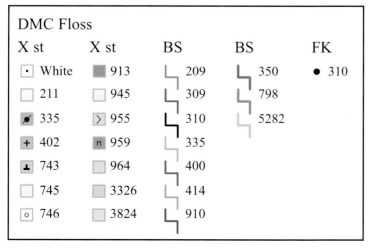

DMC Floss

X st		X st		BS		BS		FK	
·	White		913	∟	209	∟	350	●	310
	211		945	∟	309	∟	798		
✗	335	>	955	∟	310	∟	5282		
+	402	n	959	∟	335				
⊥	743		964	∟	400				
	745		3326	∟	414				
○	746		3824	∟	910				

bootie
Stitch Count: 7 width x 9 length

White hooded bath towel (as shown on page 17)

Stitch Count: 110 width x 93 length

left

Blue Gingham ball cap (as shown on page 17)
Stitch Count: 34 width x 45 length

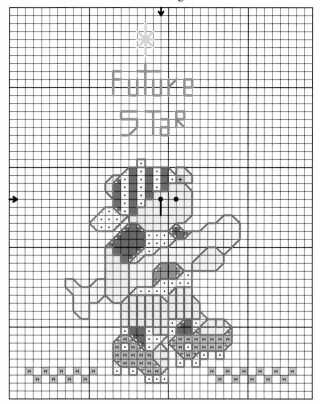

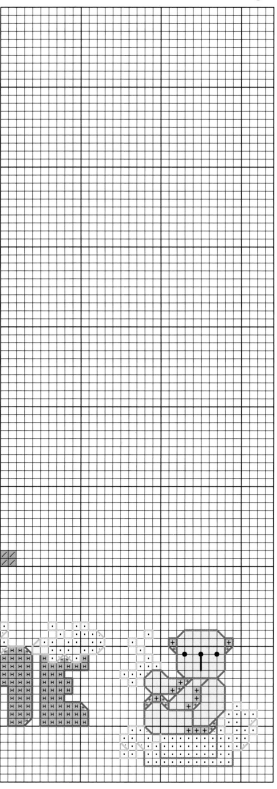

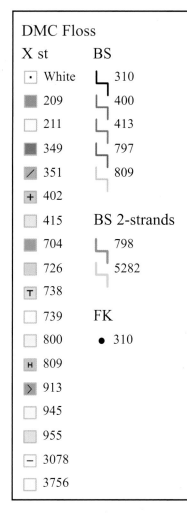

DMC Floss			
X st		**BS**	
· White		310	
209		400	
211		413	
349		797	
/ 351		809	
+ 402			
415		**BS 2-strands**	
704		798	
726		5282	
T 738			
739		**FK**	
800		● 310	
H 809			
＞ 913			
945			
955			
− 3078			
3756			

cup
Stitch Count: 74 width x 23 length

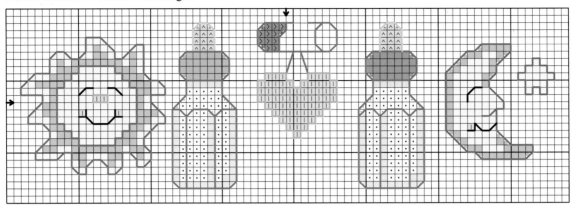

Star & Bear burp towel (as shown on page 17)
Stitch Count: 69 width x 19 length

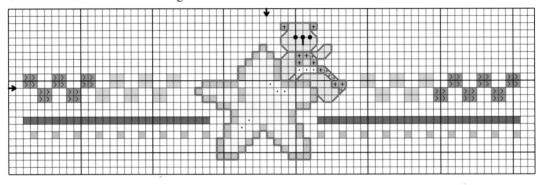

Sun & Bear visor (as shown on page 17)
Stitch Count: 24 width x 18 length

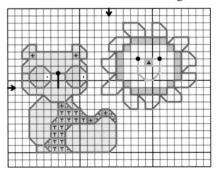

ball cap
Stitch Count: 24 width x 41 length

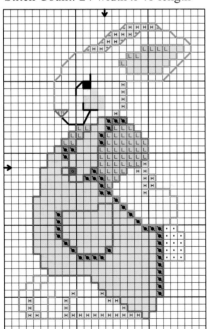

DMC Floss				
X st	X st	X st	BS	BS
· White	726	o 958	309	3341
210	746	959	310	FK
■ 310	799	T 964	400	• 310
350	800	3078	413	
+ 402	913	3708	435	
415	945	3713	602	
I 605	955	∧ 3824	797	
H 677	L 957		958	

BATH TIME

Future STAR

A STAR IS BORN

I'm a STAR

Hearts & Flowers hooded towel (as shown on page 19)
Stitch Count: 175 width x 20 length

left

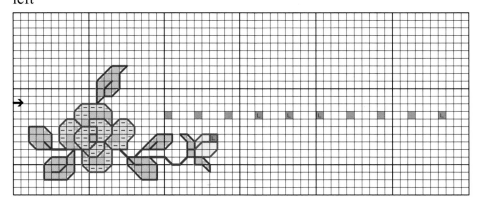

center

right

Hearts & Flowers bath mitt (as shown on page 19)
Stitch Count: 71 width x 17 length

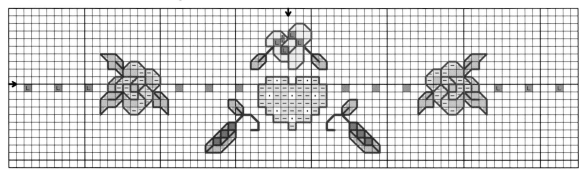

DMC Floss
X st
· White
☐ 745
☐ 799
– 818
☐ 913
☐ 955
☐ 3326
L 3825
BS
309
910
3826
BS 2-strands
911

Hearts & Flowers round bib (as shown above)
Stitch Count: 99 width x 15 length

left

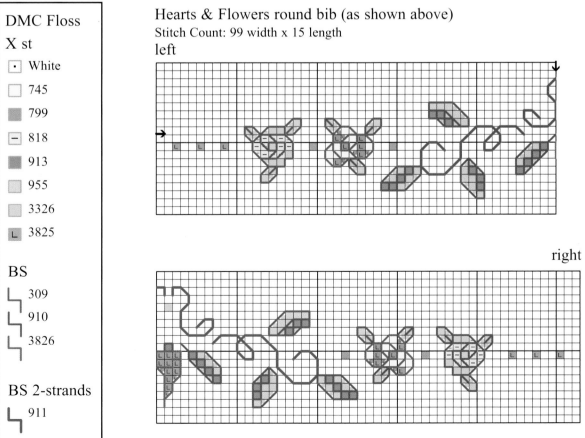

right

Hearts & Flowers square bib (as shown on page 19)
Stitch Count: 136 width x 16 length
left

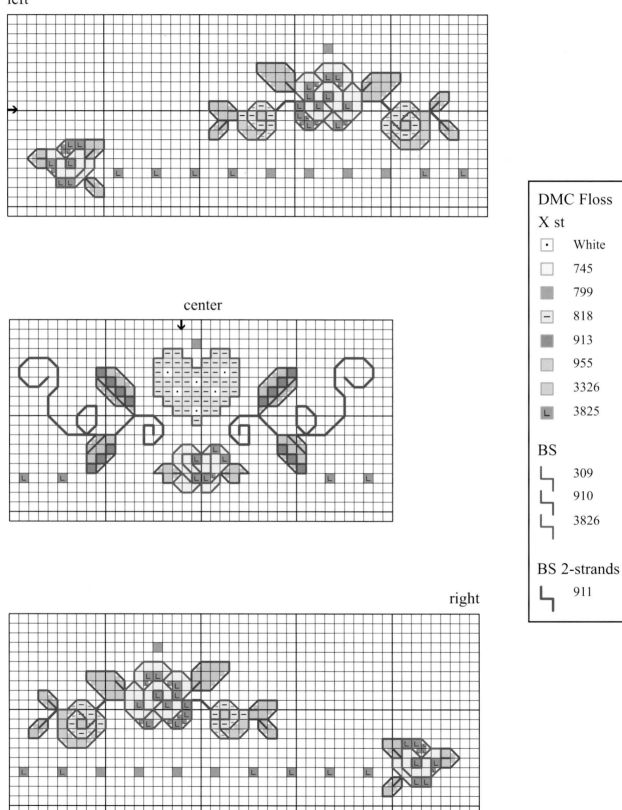

center

right

DMC Floss
X st

·	White
	745
	799
−	818
	913
	955
	3326
L	3825

BS

L	309
L	910
L	3826

BS 2-strands

L	911

bath towel
Stitch Count: 76 width x 64 length

bootie
Stitch Count: 11 width x 17 length

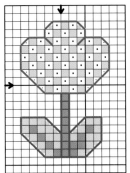

mitten
Stitch Count: 21 width x 15 length

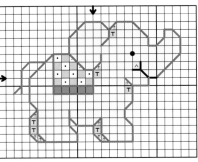

DMC Floss						
X st	X st	X st	X st	BS	BS	FK
· White	T 415	■ 798	955	⌐ 309	⌐ 413	● 310
Ɪ 304	■ 666	∧ 818	□ 3078	⌐ 310	⌐ 798	
■ 310	− 726	913	3326	⌐ 400	⌐ 910	
+ 402	□ 762	945	/ 3776			

numbers

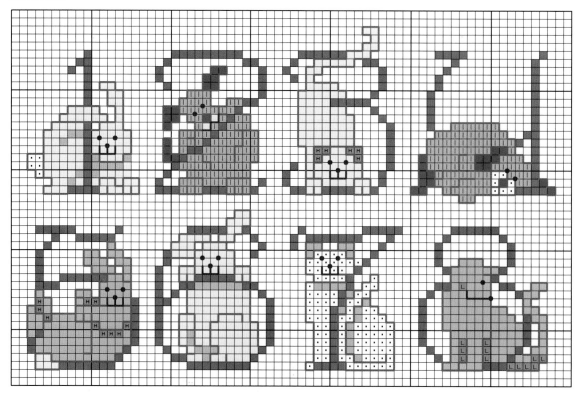

bib
Stitch Count: 34 width x 35 length

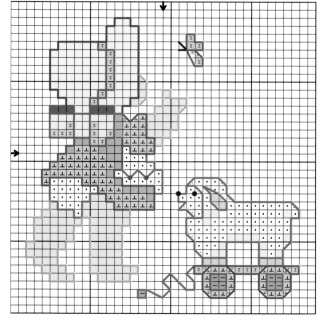

Stitch Count: 64 width x 60 length

Stitch Count: 39 width x 36 length

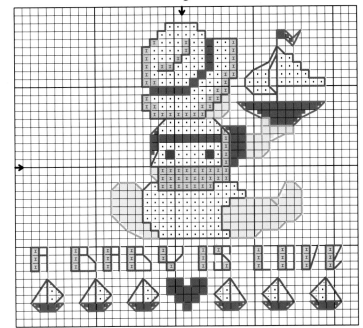

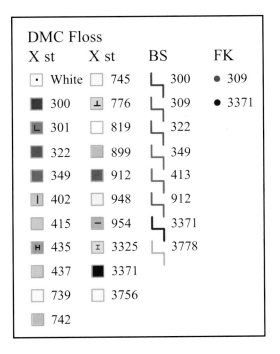

DMC Floss			
X st	X st	BS	FK
· White	745	⌐ 300	● 309
■ 300	⊥ 776	⌐ 309	● 3371
∟ 301	819	⌐ 322	
■ 322	899	⌐ 349	
349	912	⌐ 413	
I 402	948	⌐ 912	
415	− 954	⌐ 3371	
H 435	I 3325	⌐ 3778	
437	■ 3371		
739	3756		
742			

Stitch Count: 47 width x 46 length

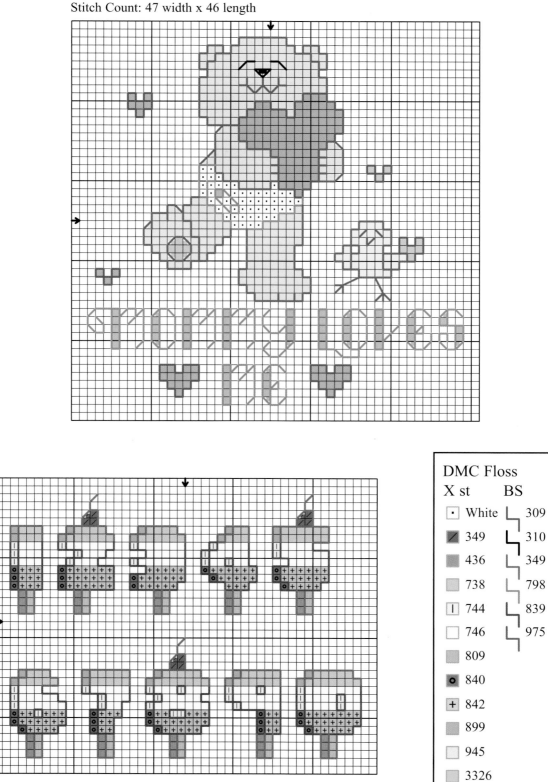

DMC Floss

X st		BS	
·	White	⌐	309
◢	349	⌐	310
	436	⌐	349
	738	⌐	798
I	744	⌐	839
	746	⌐	975
	809		
◉	840		
+	842		
	899		
	945		
	3326		

Stitch Count: 70 width x 49 length

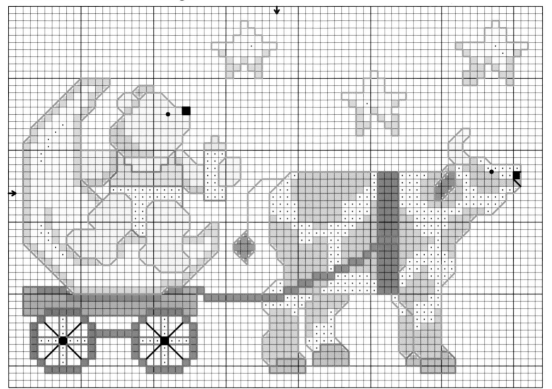

Stitch Count: 48 width x 57 length

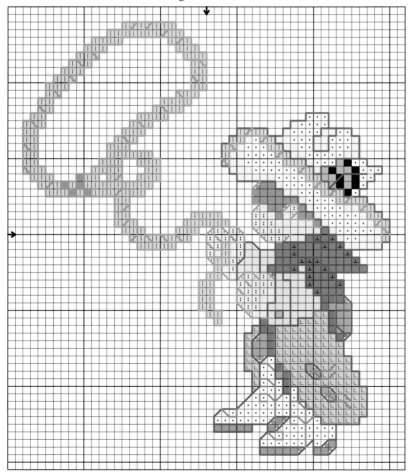

DMC Floss		
X st	X st	BS
· White	813	⌐ 301
209	826	⌐ 310
301	912	⌐ 666
⊥ 304	945	⌐ 3799
■ 310	: 951	
318	958	FK
402	964	● 310
666	3078	
726	3824	
L 738	I 3827	
775		

25

Designs for Pillows

To the Beach pillow (as shown on page 27)
Stitch Count: 81 width x 71 length

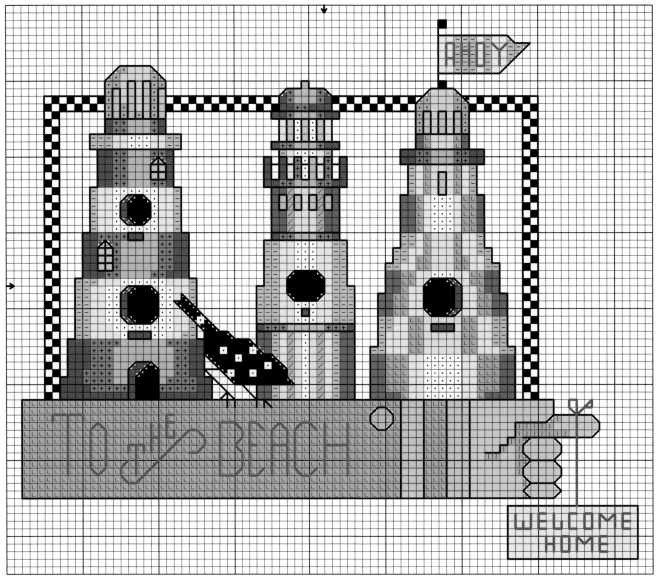

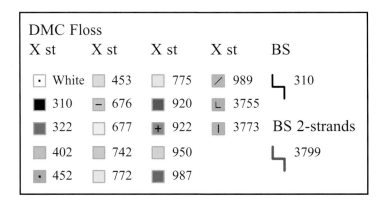

DMC Floss				
X st	X st	X st	X st	BS
· White	453	775	/ 989	⌐ 310
■ 310	− 676	920	L 3755	
322	677	+ 922	I 3773	BS 2-strands
402	742	950		⌐ 3799
· 452	772	987		

Sunflower pillow (as shown on page 26)
Stitch Count: 51 width x 73 length

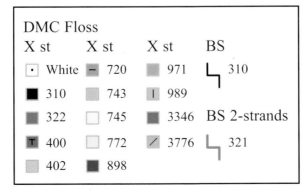

DMC Floss			
X st	X st	X st	BS
· White	— 720	971	⌐ 310
■ 310	743	I 989	
▒ 322	□ 745	3346	BS 2-strands
T 400	772	╱ 3776	⌐ 321
402	▓ 898		

Stitch Count: 38 width x 48 length

Stitch Count: 36 width x 46 length

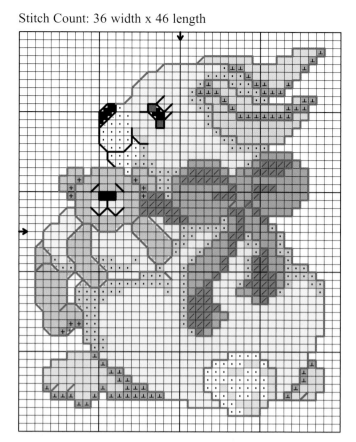

Stitch Count: 41 width x 52 length

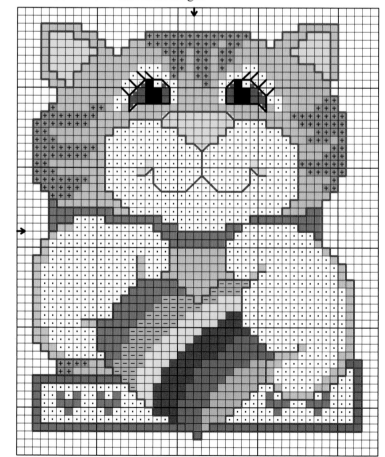

DMC Floss		
X st	X st	BS
· White	· 738	⌐ 310
+ 301	□ 739	⌐ 3799
■ 310	− 740	
▦ 321	▨ 741	
▦ 402	□ 743	
⊥ 414	▦ 776	
▦ 415	▦ 826	
■ 433	╱ 958	
▦ 700	▦ 959	
▦ 718		

Stitch Count: 69 width x 85 length

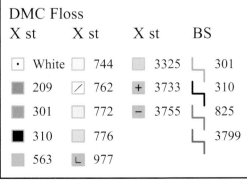

DMC Floss			
X st	X st	X st	BS
· White	744	+ 3733	301
209	762	− 3755	310
301	772		825
310	776		3799
563	L 977		

Stitch Count: 52 width x 45 length

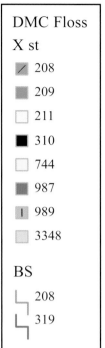

DMC Floss

X st

/ 208

■ 209

□ 211

■ 310

□ 744

■ 987

I 989

□ 3348

BS

⌐ 208

⌐ 319

Victorian pillow (as shown on page 32)
Stitch Count: 60 width x 83 length

DMC Floss

X st		X st		X st		X st		X st		X st		BS		BS	
·	White	■	319	I	603	╱	772	–	971	+	3755	└	208	└	825
■	208	■	321	■	604		775		977	■	3812	└	310	└	900
❯	209	■	322	╱	606		900	L	987	·	3817	└	600	└	986
	211	I	502		742	⊥	958		989		3826	└	742		
■	310	■	600		744	■	959	·	3689						

33

Birdhouse pillow (as shown on page 35)
Stitch Count: 58 width x 84 length

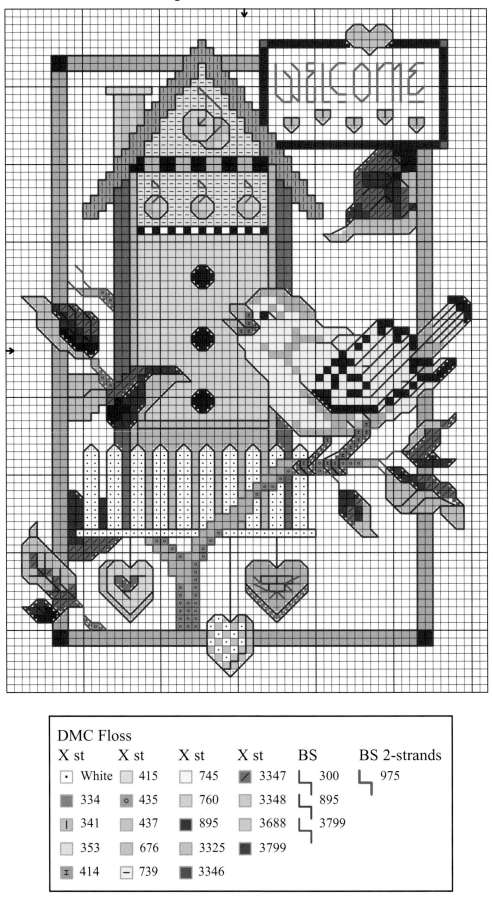

DMC Floss					
X st	X st	X st	X st	BS	BS 2-strands
· White	▨ 415	▢ 745	▨ 3347	⌐ 300	⌐ 975
▨ 334	○ 435	▨ 760	▨ 3348	⌐ 895	
I 341	▨ 437	■ 895	▨ 3688	⌐ 3799	
▨ 353	▨ 676	▨ 3325	▨ 3799		
ɪ 414	– 739	▨ 3346			

Stitch Count: 50 width x 45 length

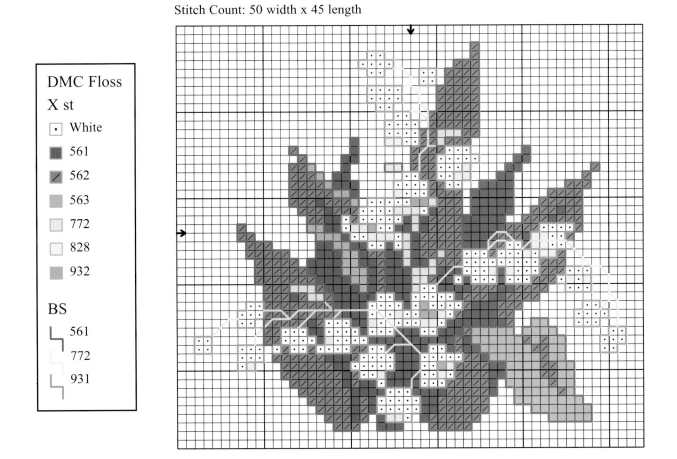

DMC Floss
X st

·	White
■	561
⧄	562
▨	563
▨	772
□	828
▨	932

BS

⌐	561
⌐	772
⌐	931

Frog pillow (as shown on page 35)
Stitch Count: 52 width x 76 length

DMC Floss

X st		X st		X st		BS		FK	
⊡	White	▨	828	■	3371	⌐	562	●	3371
▮	352	▦	906	▨	3608	⌐	699		
−	437	▨	954	⁄	3820	⌐	807		
▙	562	▨	3328	▨	3822	⌐	3371		
⌐	807	▨	3348						

Stitch Count: 57 width x 72 length

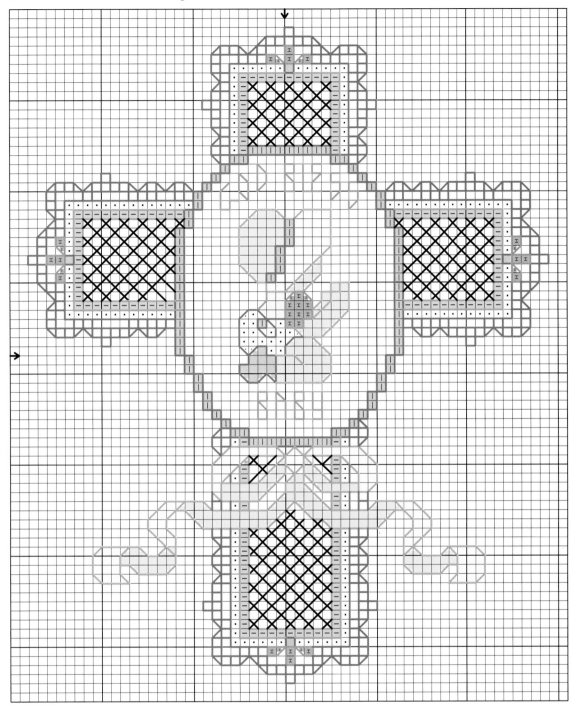

DMC Floss

X st		X st		BS		BS	
·	White	⊡	948	⌐	208	⌐	White
ɪ	210	⌶	964	⌐	958		
☐	211	☐	3823	⌐	3340		
▨	564	−	3824	⌐	3776		
☐	745						

38

Table Linens

Feather place mat (as shown on page 39)
Stitch Count: 64 width x 68 length

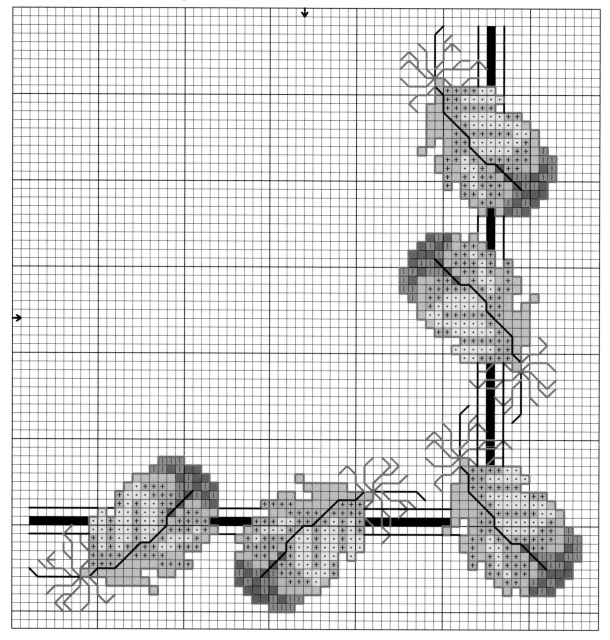

Feather napkin (as shown on page 39)
Stitch Count: 18 width x 22 length

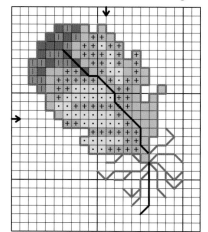

DMC Floss		
X st	X st	BS
■ 310	▨ 632	└ 310
+ 402	· 951	└ 632
I 407	▦ 3776	

Stitch Count: 69 width x 69 length

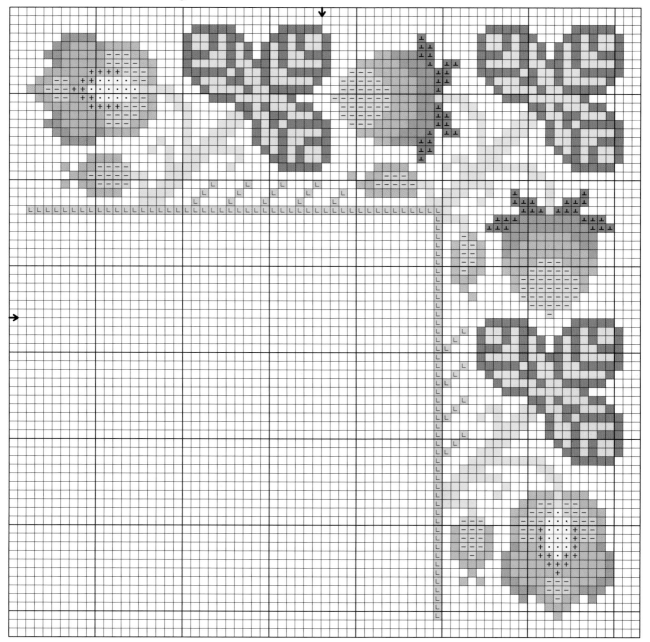

Stitch Count: 34 width x 21 length

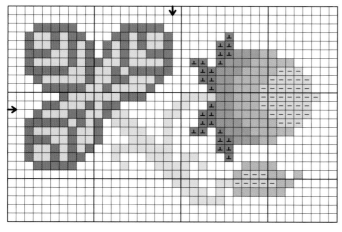

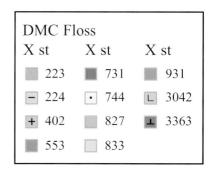

DMC Floss		
X st	X st	X st
▧ 223	▨ 731	▨ 931
▬ 224	· 744	L 3042
+ 402	▨ 827	⊥ 3363
▨ 553	▨ 833	

41

Stitch Count: 42 width x 60 length

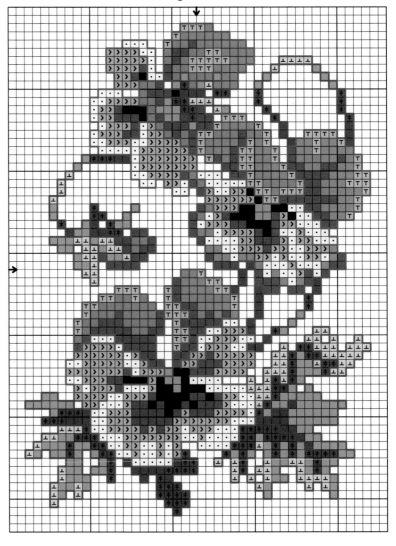

DMC Floss

X st		X st		BS	
■	310	✸	987	⌐	310
■	333	▨	989	⌐	333
⌐	340	▨	993	⌐	550
■	550	·	3078	⌐	920
▨	721	▨	3607	⌐	986
⊥	772	T	3608	⌐	991
−	964	▨	3747		
❭	972	■	3803		
▨	986	I	3814		

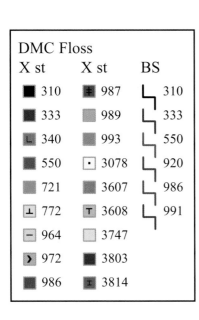

Pansy place mat (as shown on page 39)
Stitch Count: 39 width x 33 length

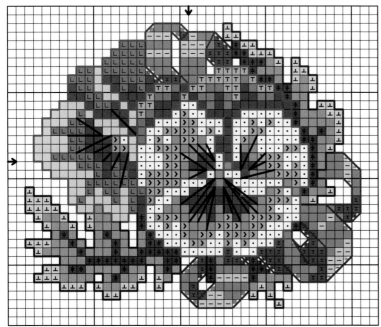

Pansy napkin (as shown on page 39)
Stitch Count: 22 width x 24 length

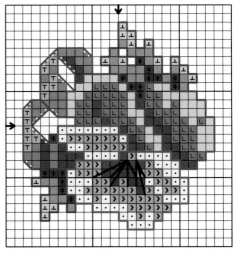

Stitch Count: 16 width x 34 length

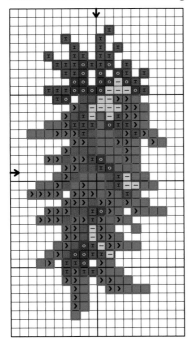

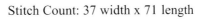

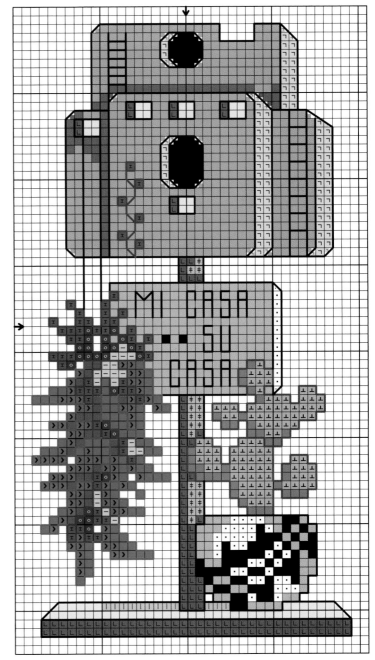

DMC Floss

X st		X st		BS	
·	White		677	⌐	310
■	310	■	815	⌐	815
❯	321	◉	890	⌐	890
⌐	353	ᴵ	987		
■	355	−	3348		
L	400	‡	3776		
	648		3778		
■	666	■	3816		
I	676	⊥	3817		

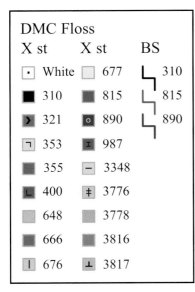

Stitch Count: 70 width x 69 length

Stitch Count: 28 width x 24 length

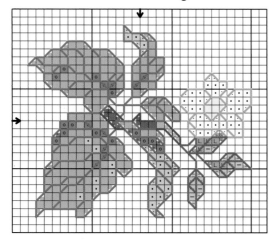

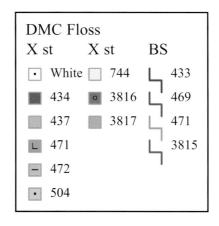

DMC Floss		
X st	X st	BS
· White	☐ 744	⌐ 433
■ 434	o 3816	⌐ 469
▨ 437	▨ 3817	⌐ 471
L 471		⌐ 3815
– 472		
· 504		

44

Butterfly place mat (as shown on page 39)
Stitch Count: 39 width x 51 length

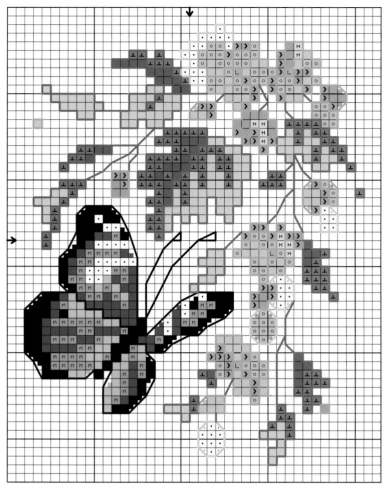

Butterfly napkin
(as shown on page 39)
Stitch Count: 17 width x 19 length

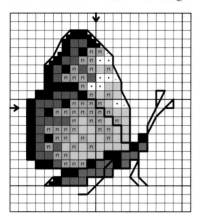

Stitch Count: 28 width x 67 length

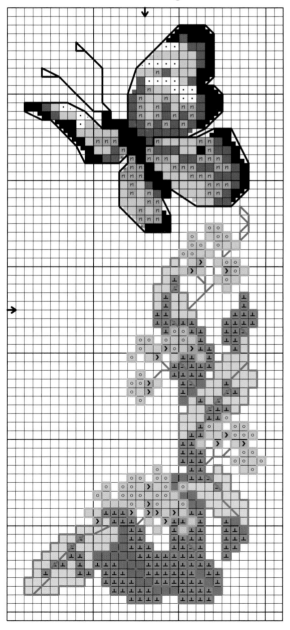

DMC Floss

X st		X st	
·	White	❭	3705
■	310		3706
	352	o	3708
H	353	⊥	3816
	501		
L	729	**BS**	
	742	L	310
	772	L	501
·	819	L	975
	920	L	3705
n	971	L	3706
	975		

Stitch Count: 61 width x 62 length

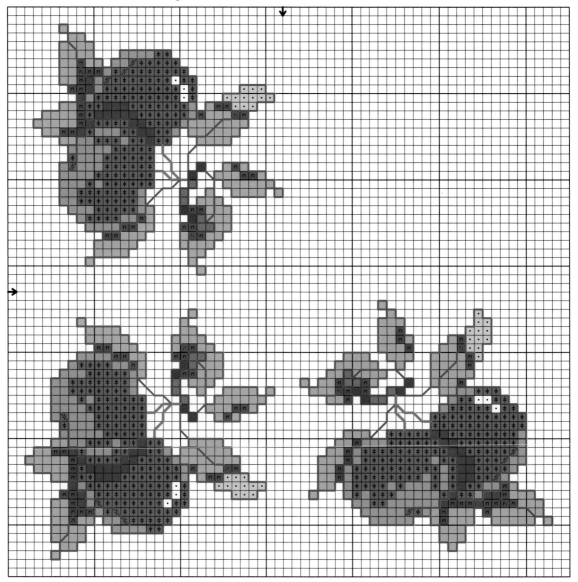

Stitch Count: 16 width x 14 length

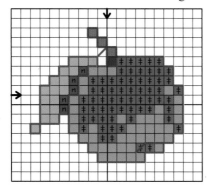

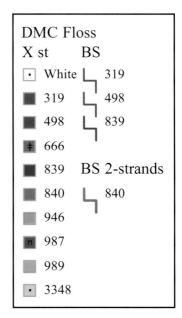

DMC Floss

X st		BS	
·	White		319
■	319		498
■	498		839
‡	666		
■	839	BS 2-strands	
■	840		840
■	946		
n	987		
■	989		
·	3348		

Stitch Count: 30 width x 30 length

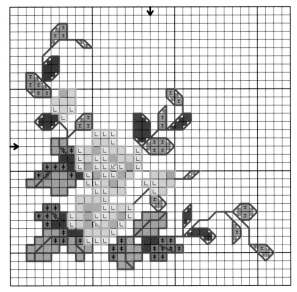

Eat Dessert First place mat (as shown on page 38)
Stitch Count: 38 width x 50 length

DMC Floss

X st		X st		BS	
·	White		800	⌐	310
	210	T	809	⌐	335
■	310	L	818	⌐	400
	335	■	905	⌐	437
+	402		945	⌐	561
	434	⊥	959	⌐	905
I	471		3817	⌐	3810
‡	502	·	3823		
	561			**BS 2-strands**	
	745			⌐	597
	776				

Eat Dessert First napkin
(as shown on page 38)
Stitch Count: 20 width x 18 length

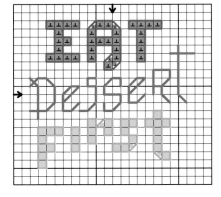

Stitch Count: 44 width x 29 length

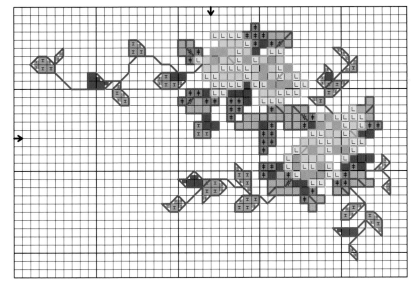

Red Berries place mat (as shown on page 38)
Stitch Count: 65 width x 59 length

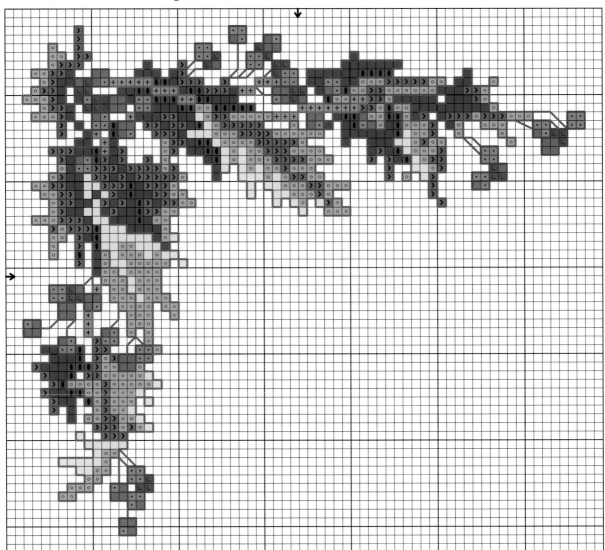

Red Berries napkin
(as shown on page 38)
Stitch Count: 18 width x 17 length

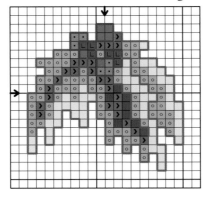

Stitch Count: 42 width x 68 length

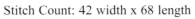

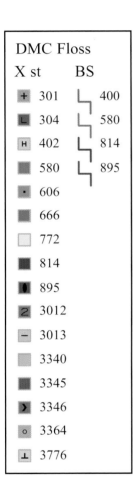

DMC Floss

X st		BS	
+	301	⌐	400
L	304	⌐	580
H	402	⌐	814
	580	⌐	895
·	606		
	666		
	772		
	814		
	895		
2	3012		
−	3013		
	3340		
	3345		
⟩	3346		
o	3364		
⊥	3776		

Designs

for Towels

Violin towel (as shown on page 51)
Stitch Count: 54 width x 30 length

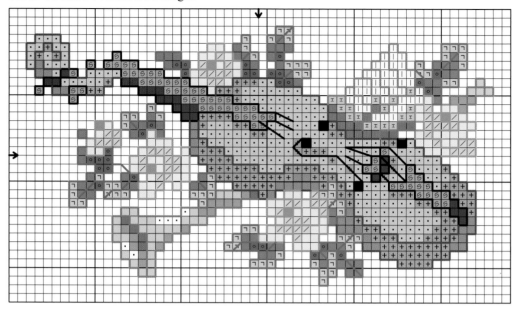

Stitch Count: 71 width x 25 length

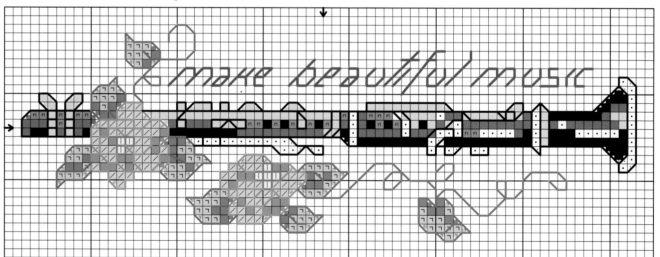

Stitch Count: 75 width x 21 length

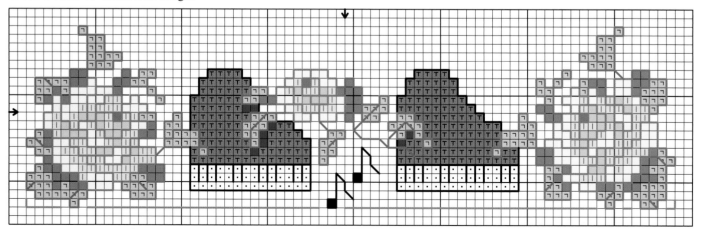

Welcome fingertip towel (as shown on page 51)
Stitch Count: 54 width x 25 length

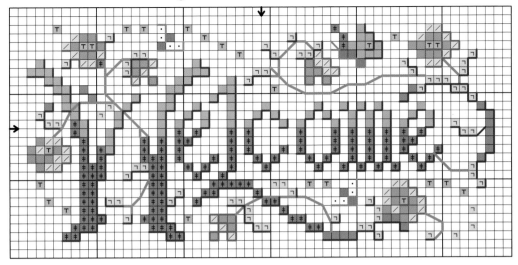

Hibiscus fingertip towel (as shown on page 51)
Stitch Count: 56 width x 28 length

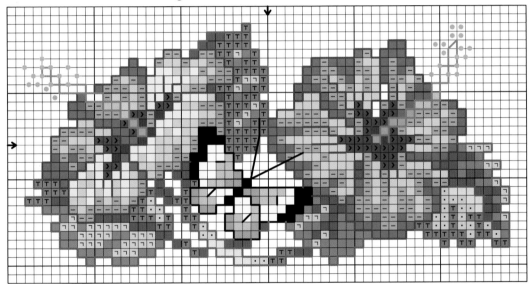

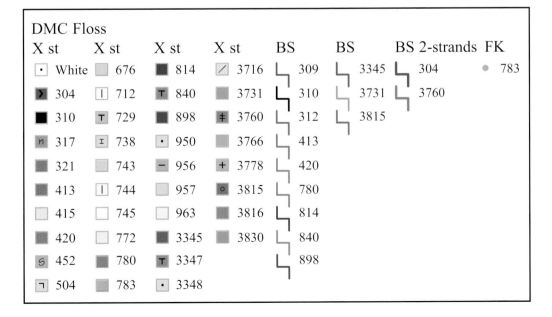

DMC Floss							
X st	X st	X st	X st	BS	BS	BS 2-strands	FK
White	676	814	3716	309	3345	304	783
304	712	840	309	310	3731	3760	
310	729	898	310	312	3815		
317	738	950	3760	413			
321	743	956	3766	420			
413	744	957	3778	780			
415	745	963	3815	814			
420	772	3345	3816	840			
452	780	3347	3830	898			
504	783	3348					

Stitch Count: 51 width x 21 length

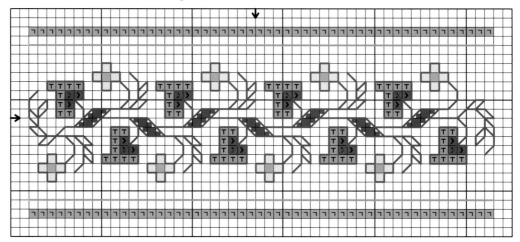

Grapes fingertip towel (as shown on page 51)
Stitch Count: 56 width x 31 length

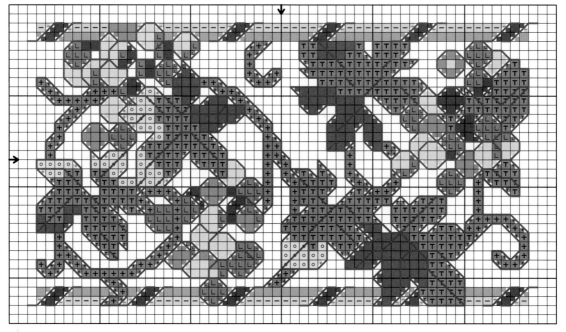

Stitch Count: 58 width x 23 length

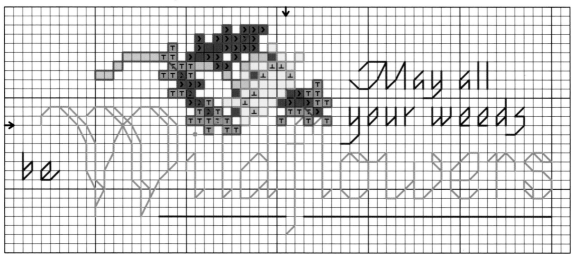

Stitch Count: 80 width x 28 length

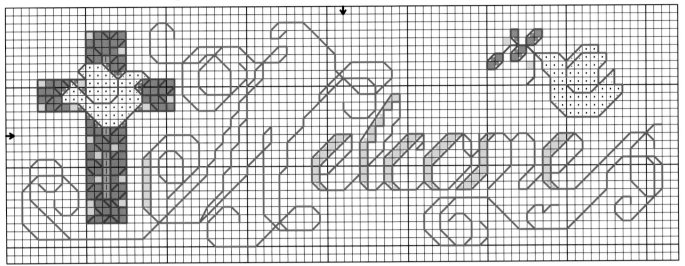

Daisy fingertip towel (as shown on page 51)
Stitch Count: 77 width x 30 length

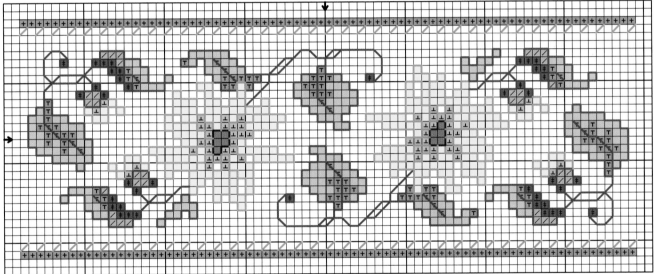

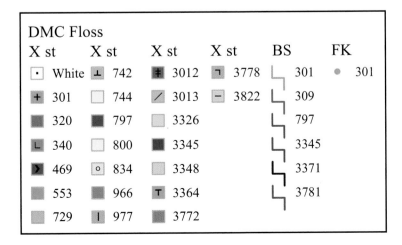

DMC Floss

X st	X st	X st	X st	BS	FK
· White	⊥ 742	‡ 3012	⌐ 3778	└ 301	● 301
+ 301	☐ 744	╱ 3013	− 3822	└ 309	
▦ 320	▪ 797	▨ 3326		└ 797	
∟ 340	☐ 800	▪ 3345		└ 3345	
▶ 469	○ 834	▨ 3348		└ 3371	
▦ 553	▨ 966	T 3364		└ 3781	
▨ 729	∣ 977	▨ 3772			

Stitch Count: 114 width x 29 length
left

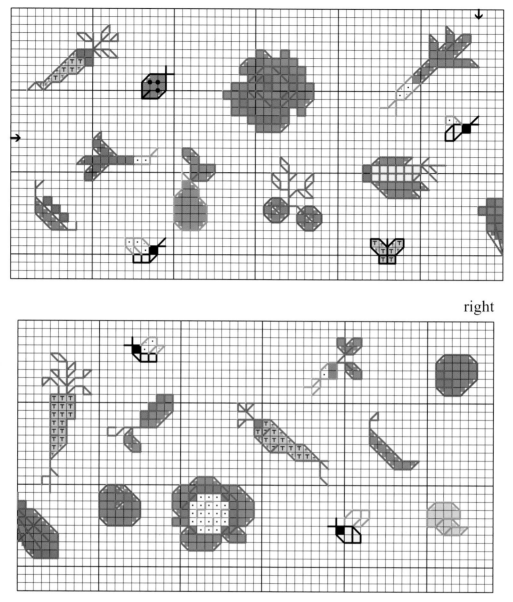

right

Stitch Count: 62 width x 24 length

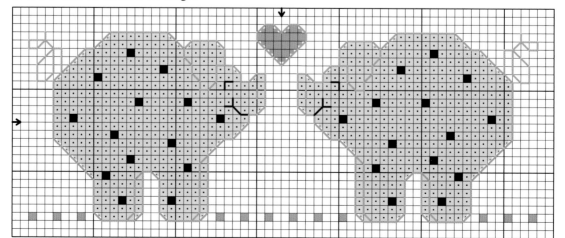

Seasons Greetings fingertip towel (as shown on page 51)
Stitch Count: 72 width x 30 length

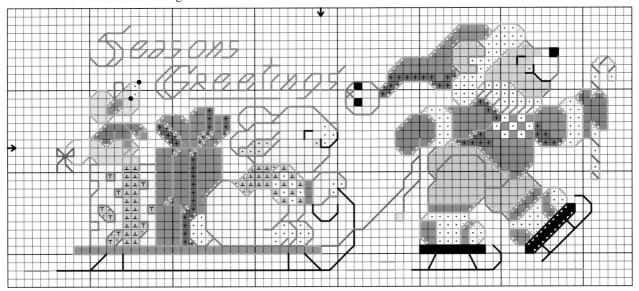

Stitch Count: 64 width x 31 length

DMC Floss						
X st	X st	X st	X st	BS	BS	FK
· White	T 722	966	· 3716	⌐ 310	⌐ 961	• 310
■ 310	739	988	3799	⌐ 317	⌐ 986	
317	744	− 993	3827	⌐ 400	⌐ 996	
+ 321	754	996		⌐ 700	⌐ 3799	
400	ɪ 809	3325		⌐ 809		
553	912	n 3326		⌐ 816		
606	o 943	ǀ 3341		⌐ 943		
644	961	⊥ 3608				

Cookies potholder (as shown on page 50)
Stitch Count: 43 width x 41 length

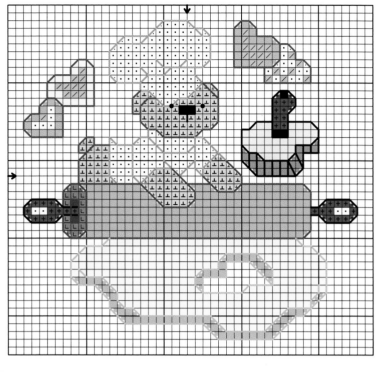

Peas Porridge potholder (as shown on page 50)
Stitch Count: 52 width x 54 length

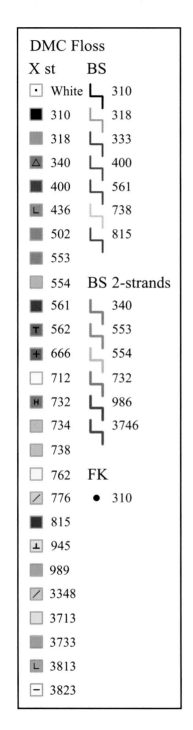

DMC Floss		
X st	**BS**	
· White	⌐ 310	
■ 310	⌐ 318	
■ 318	⌐ 333	
△ 340	⌐ 400	
■ 400	⌐ 561	
L 436	⌐ 738	
■ 502	⌐ 815	
■ 553		
■ 554	**BS 2-strands**	
■ 561	⌐ 340	
T 562	⌐ 553	
+ 666	⌐ 554	
□ 712	⌐ 732	
H 732	⌐ 986	
· 734	⌐ 3746	
■ 738		
□ 762	**FK**	
⁄ 776	● 310	
■ 815		
⊥ 945		
■ 989		
⁄ 3348		
□ 3713		
■ 3733		
L 3813		
− 3823		

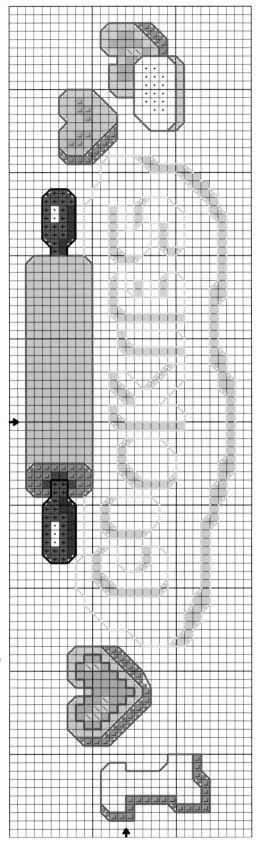

Cookies kitchen towel (as shown on page 50)
Stitch Count: 96 width x 25 length

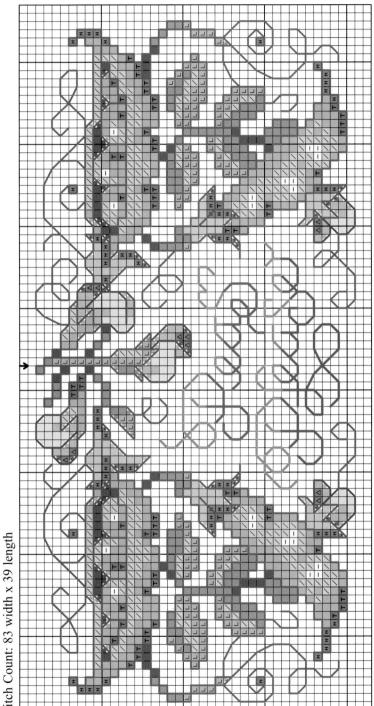

Peas Please kitchen towel (as shown on page 50)
Stitch Count: 83 width x 39 length

Designs for Jar Covers and Coasters

Apple coaster (as shown on page 61)
Stitch Count: 27 width x 29 length

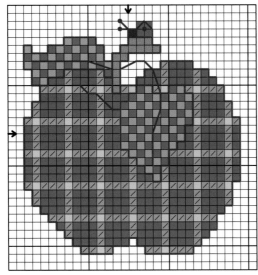

Cherries coaster (as shown on page 61)
Stitch Count: 30 width x 28 length

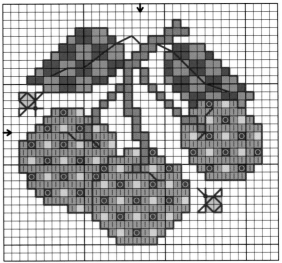

Watermelon jar cover (as shown on page 60)
Stitch Count: 25 width x 28 length

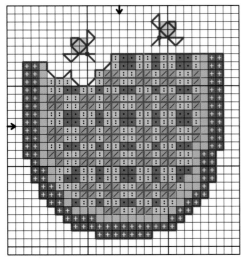

Pear coaster (as shown on page 60)
Stitch Count: 26 width x 27 length

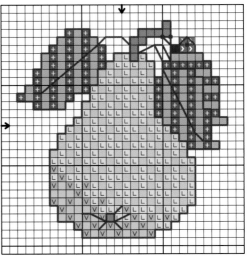

Pumpkin jar cover (as shown on page 61)
Stitch Count: 29 width x 29 length

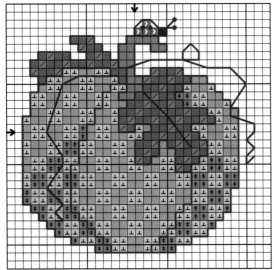

Carrots jar cover (as shown on page 61)
Stitch Count: 25 width x 29 length

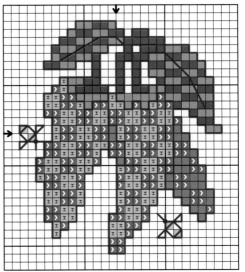

DMC Floss

X st	X st	X st
· White	· 746	989
301	− 760	H 3326
◎ 304	817	V 3340
309	□ 818	3341
■ 349	824	I 3706
⁄ 351	826	⊥ 3825
∶ 353	827	
552	899	BS
I 602	905	└ 304
604	⁄ 906	└ 938
❯ 666	907	
✚ 720	◉ 911	FK
721	■ 938	● 938
743	· 954	
L 744	✚ 987	

Heart jar cover (as shown on page 61)
Stitch Count: 28 width x 28 length

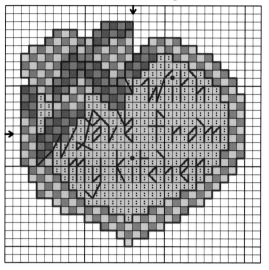

Strawberry jar cover (as shown on page 67)
Stitch Count: 24 width x 28 length

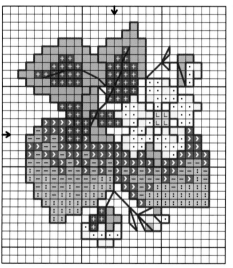

Sugar 'n Spice jar cover (as shown on page 60)
Stitch Count: 27 width x 26 length

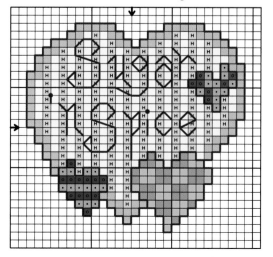

jar cover
Stitch Count: 26 width x 29 length

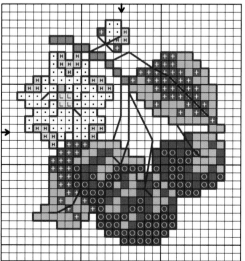

jar cover
Stitch Count: 29 width x 26 length

jar cover
Stitch Count: 25 width x 26 length

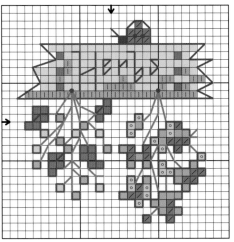

Fruit jar cover (as shown on page 60)
Stitch Count: 28 width x 29 length

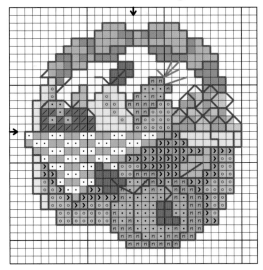

jar cover
Stitch Count: 27 width x 26 length

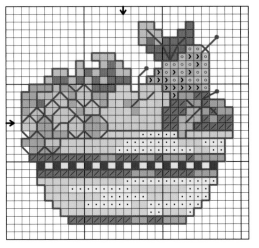

coaster
Stitch Count: 35 width x 33 length

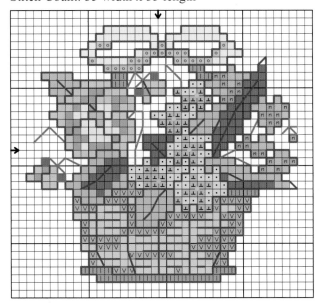

coaster
Stitch Count: 33 width x 34 length

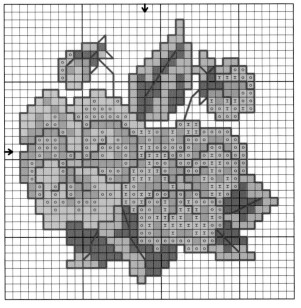

coaster
Stitch Count: 42 width x 42 length

DMC Floss

X st		X st	
· White			813
	210		826
+	347		938
/	349	⊥	962
	351		987
−	518		989
	519	↑	3328
	553	I	3608
	676	·	3716
·	677	**BS**	
I	680	⌐	938
n	721	⌐	987
	722		
o	725	**FK**	
	727	·	351
V	729	·	518
·	741	·	553
L	760	·	725
›	783	●	938

coaster
Stitch Count: 41 width x 40 length

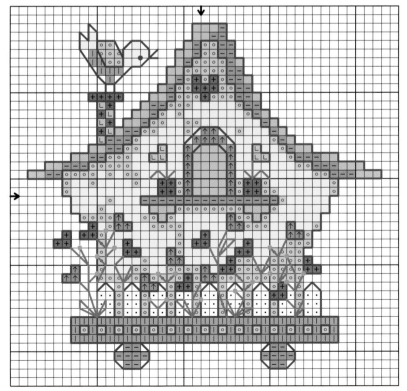

Fruit & Heart jar cover (as shown on page 67)
Stitch Count: 22 width x 27 length

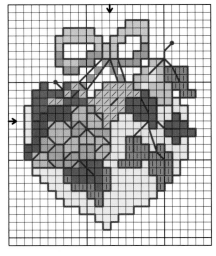

Geranium jar cover (as shown on page 67)
Stitch Count: 25 width x 28 length

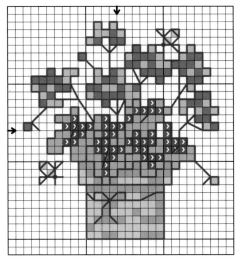

coaster
Stitch Count: 35 width x 33 length

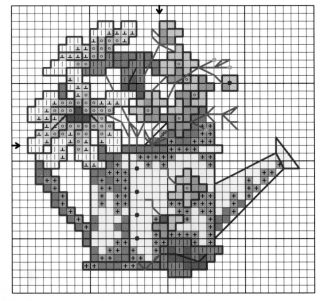

coaster
Stitch Count: 43 width x 45 length

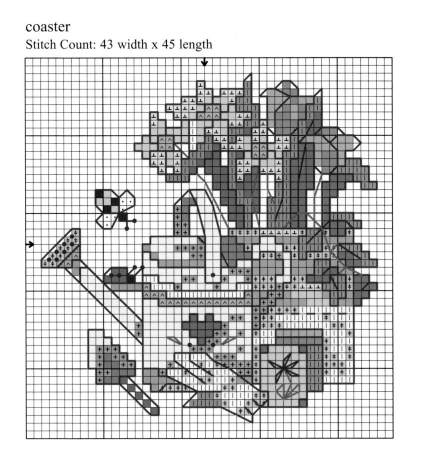

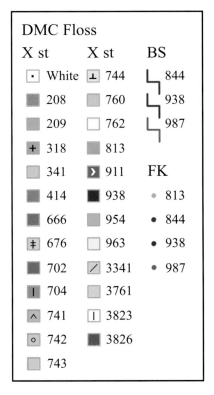

DMC Floss		
X st	X st	BS
· White	⊥ 744	844
208	760	938
209	762	987
+ 318	813	
341	❯ 911	FK
414	938	· 813
666	954	• 844
‡ 676	963	• 938
702	/ 3341	• 987
I 704	3761	
^ 741	I 3823	
o 742	3826	
743		

coaster
Stitch Count: 31 width x 33 length

coaster
Stitch Count: 40 width x 47 length

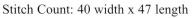

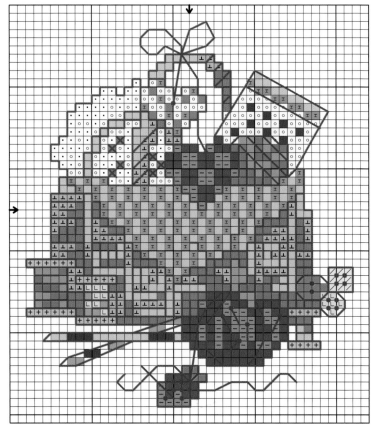

Harvest jar cover (as shown on page 67)
Stitch Count: 27 width x 29 length

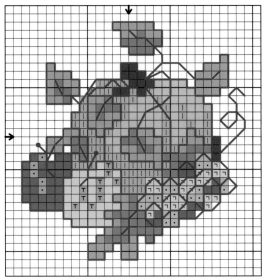

jar cover
Stitch Count: 28 width x 27 length

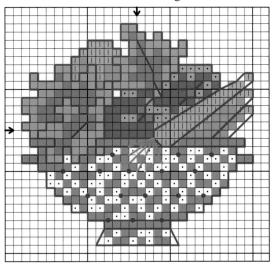

Cherry Pie jar cover (as shown on page 61)
Stitch Count: 27 width x 28 length

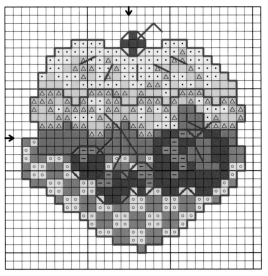

coaster
Stitch Count: 35 width x 33 length

jar cover
Stitch Count: 22 width x 26 length

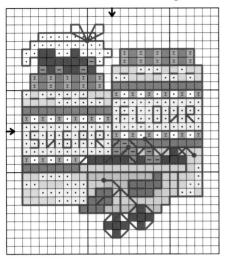

jar cover
Stitch Count: 27 width x 29 length

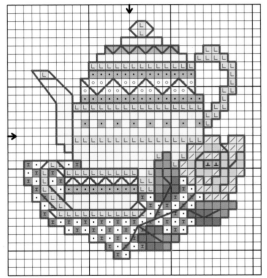

Shaker Shelf jar cover (as shown on page 61)
Stitch Count: 28 width x 26 length

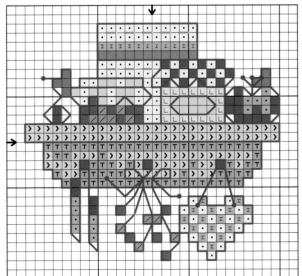

DMC Floss		
X st	X st	BS
· White	❯ 738	└ 702
⁄ 208	▦ 741	└ 826
· 209	▦ 743	└ 938
▦ 318	⁄ 744	
┐ 341	– 762	FK
– 350	I 813	● 702
· 351	▦ 817	● 938
+ 402	☐ 818	
▦ 420	▦ 826	
T 436	☐ 827	
▦ 472	▦ 938	
☐ 676	▦ 958	
· 677	▦ 961	
▦ 702	L 3716	
▦ 704	▦ 3746	
▦ 720	○ 3823	
I 721	△ 3827	
⊥ 729		

coaster
Stitch Count: 35 width x 35 length

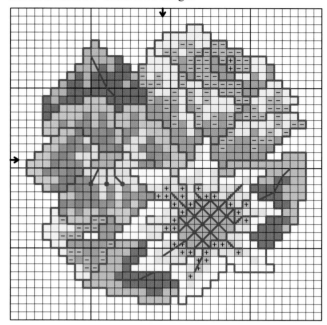

coaster
Stitch Count: 35 width x 33 length

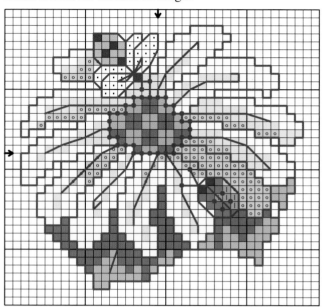

coaster
Stitch Count: 42 width x 42 length

DMC Floss		
X st	X st	X st
· White	○ 743	3776
208	744	▌ 3801
╱ 209	813	☐ 3823
210	826	
349	938	BS
· 352	961	└ 938
400	− 962	
· 676	963	FK
+ 729	987	● 938
742	989	

coaster
Stitch Count: 36 width x 30 length

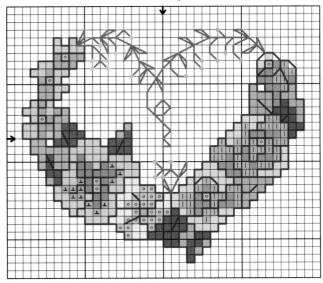

coaster
Stitch Count: 32 width x 32 length

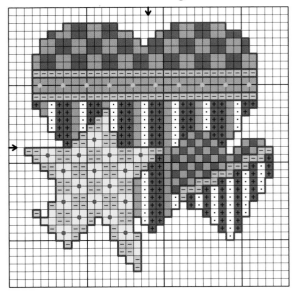

coaster
Stitch Count: 32 width x 33 length

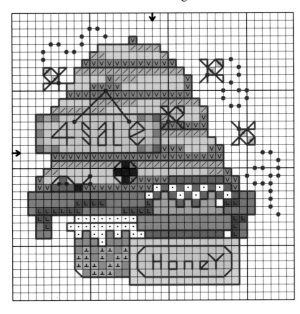

coaster
Stitch Count: 32 width x 34 length

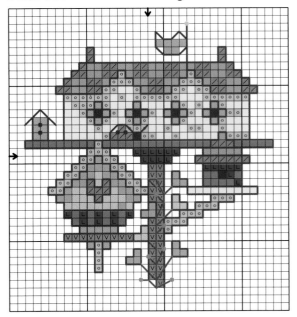

DMC Floss					
X st	X st	X st	X st	BS	FK
⊡ White	676	813	987	⌐ 700	● 209
208	∟ 700	+ 817	989	⌐ 938	● 350
⊥ 209	703	825	3716	⌐ 987	● 725
211	721	827	▭ 3820		● 813
349	∘ 725	938	∨ 3829		● 825
╱ 350	727	961			● 938
351	╱ 729	Ɩ 962			● 962
					● 3820

coaster
Stitch Count: 41 width x 41 length

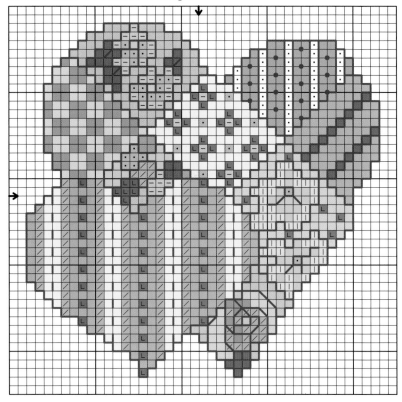

jar cover
Stitch Count: 27 width x 25 length

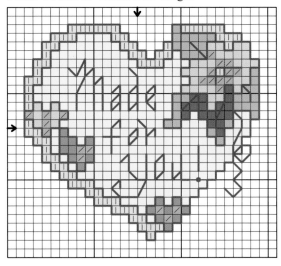

coaster
Stitch Count: 45 width x 39 length

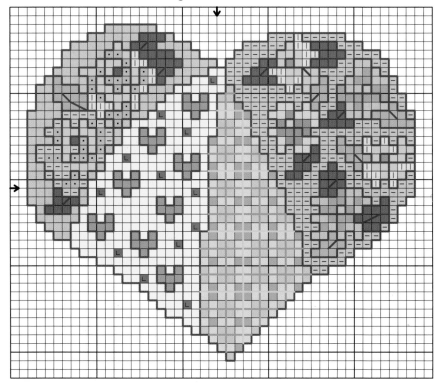

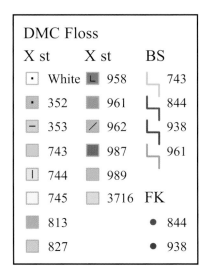

DMC Floss		
X st	X st	BS
· White	L 958	743
352	961	844
− 353	/ 962	938
743	987	961
I 744	989	
745	3716	FK
813		● 844
827		● 938

coaster
Stitch Count: 45 width x 42 length

coaster
Stitch Count: 48 width x 49 length

DMC Floss

X st   BS

209   938
301   987
721
743   FK
744   • 938
772
813
827
938
961
962
987
989
3716
3823

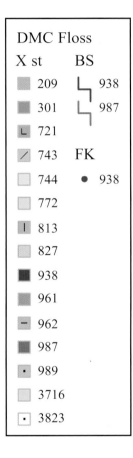
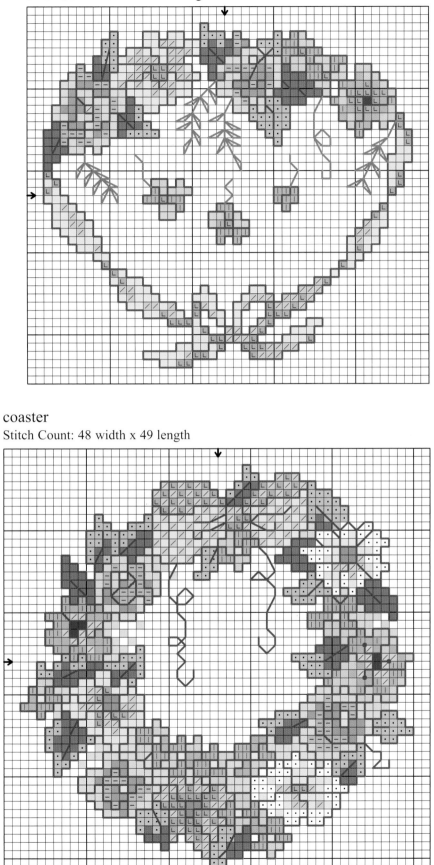

Designs for Mugs

Pagoda mug (as shown on page 74)
Stitch Count: 59 width x 42 length

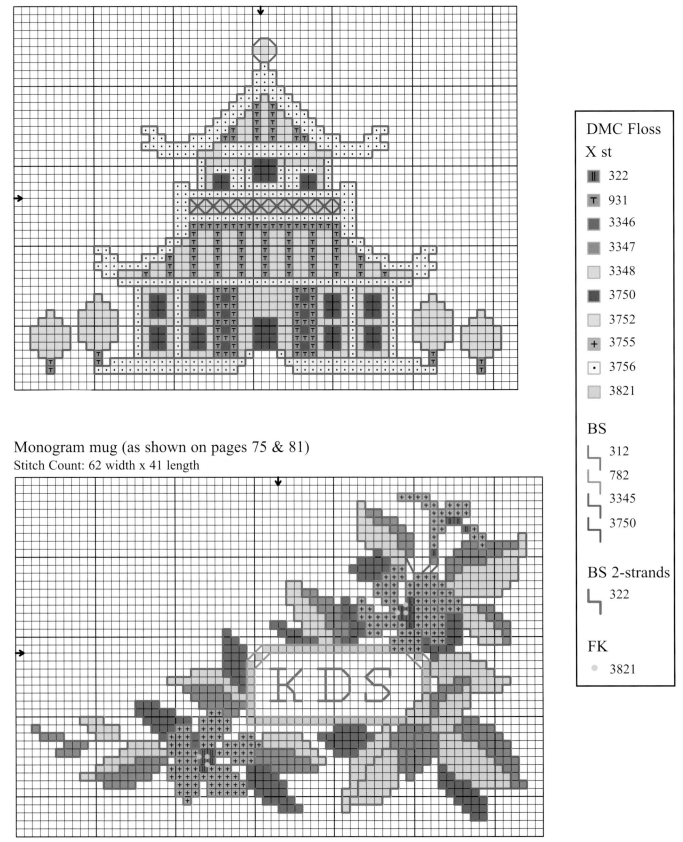

DMC Floss
X st

‖	322
T	931
■	3346
■	3347
☐	3348
■	3750
☐	3752
+	3755
·	3756
☐	3821

BS

∟	312
∟	782
∟	3345
∟	3750

BS 2-strands

∟	322

FK

•	3821

Monogram mug (as shown on pages 75 & 81)
Stitch Count: 62 width x 41 length

Stitch Count: 52 width x 45 length

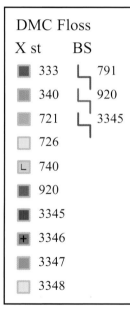

DMC Floss

X st   BS

■ 333   ⌐ 791
■ 340   ⌐ 920
■ 721   ⌐ 3345
□ 726
L 740
■ 920
■ 3345
+ 3346
■ 3347
■ 3348

Stitch Count: 50 width x 41 length

Stitch Count: 54 width x 45 length

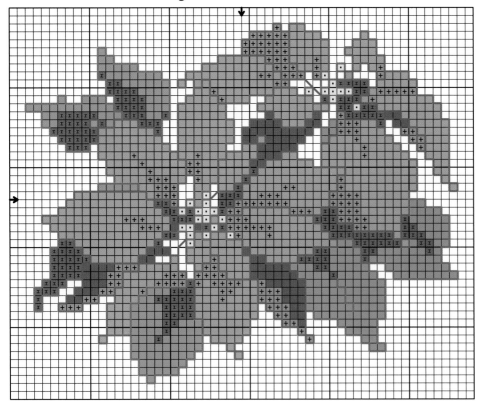

Stitch Count: 49 width x 45 length

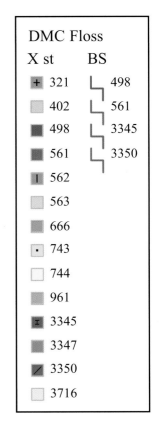

DMC Floss

X st		BS	
+	321	⌐	498
	402	⌐	561
	498	⌐	3345
	561	⌐	3350
I	562		
	563		
	666		
·	743		
	744		
	961		
I	3345		
	3347		
/	3350		
	3716		

78

Stitch Count: 59 width x 46 length

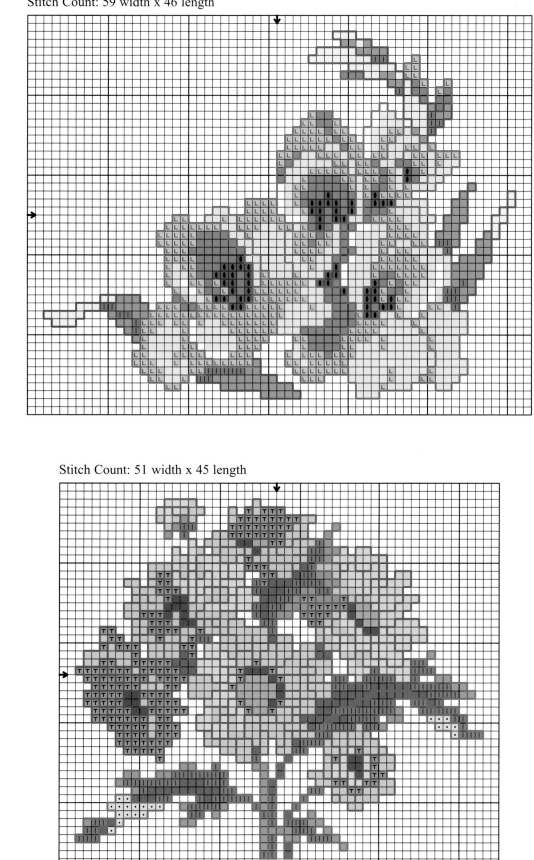

Stitch Count: 51 width x 45 length

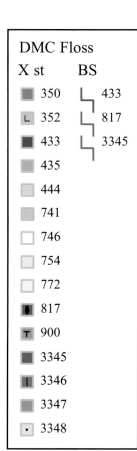

DMC Floss

X st		BS	
■	350		433
L	352		817
■	433		3345
▩	435		
▨	444		
▨	741		
☐	746		
☐	754		
☐	772		
●	817		
T	900		
■	3345		
▮	3346		
▩	3347		
·	3348		

When's Lunch? mug (as shown on page 75)
Stitch Count: 44 width x 42 length

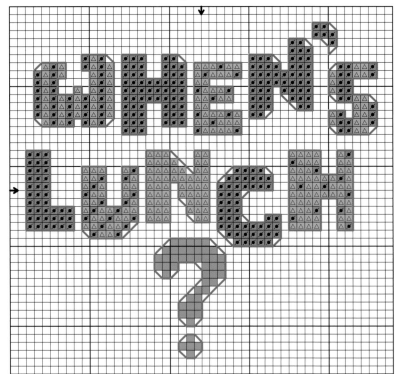

Peace and Plenty mug (as shown on pages 74 & 81)
Stitch Count: 57 width x 44 length

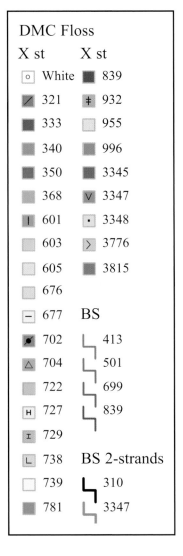

DMC Floss

X st		X st	
○	White	■	839
/	321	‡	932
■	333		955
■	340		996
■	350	■	3345
■	368	V	3347
I	601	·	3348
	603	>	3776
	605	■	3815
	676		
−	677	**BS**	
●	702	└	413
△	704	└	501
	722	└	699
H	727	└	839
I	729		
L	738	**BS 2-strands**	
	739	└	310
■	781	└	3347

MOM mug (as shown on page 81)

Stitch Count: 80 width x 24 length

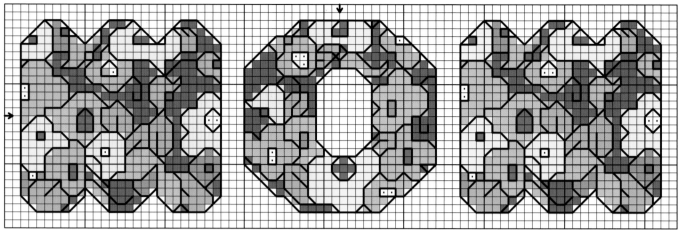

Stitch Count: 66 width x 24 length

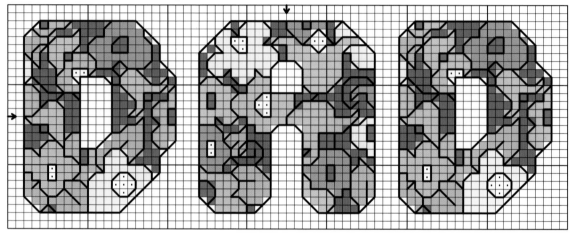

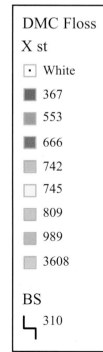

DMC Floss

X st

⊡	White
■	367
■	553
■	666
▨	742
☐	745
▨	809
▨	989
▨	3608

BS

└ 310

Stitch Count: 35 width x 23 length

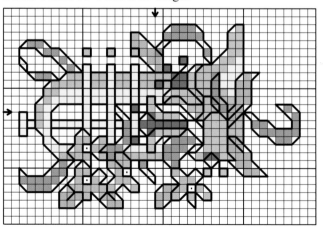

Stitch Count: 52 width x 44 length

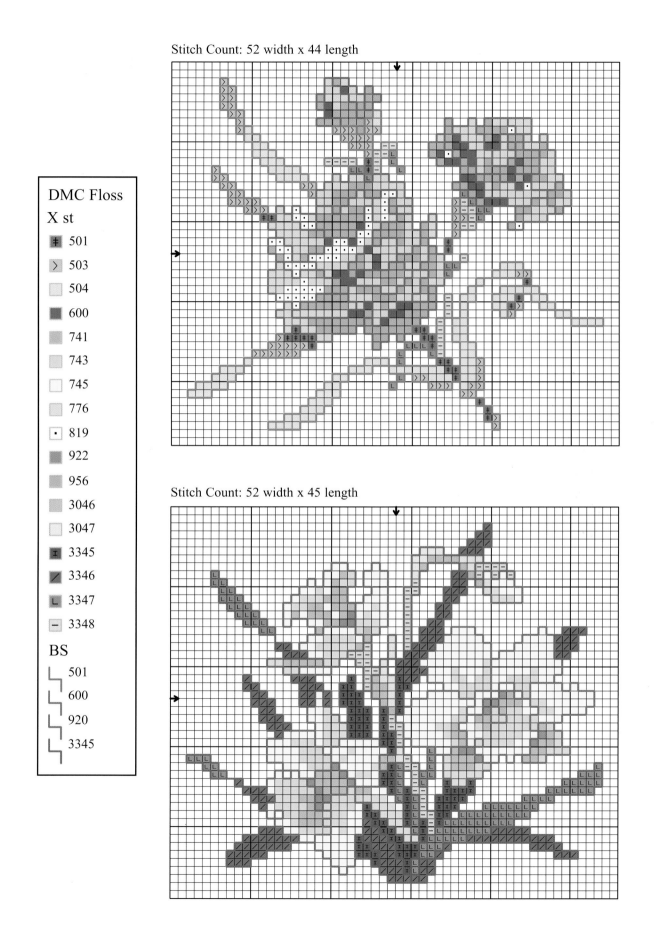

DMC Floss
X st

‡ 501
> 503
  504
  600
  741
  743
  745
  776
· 819
  922
  956
  3046
  3047
I 3345
/ 3346
L 3347
- 3348

BS
  501
  600
  920
  3345

Stitch Count: 52 width x 45 length

Teacups mug (as shown on page 75)
Stitch Count: 36 width x 41 length

Rose mug (as shown on page 75)
Stitch Count: 51 width x 43 length

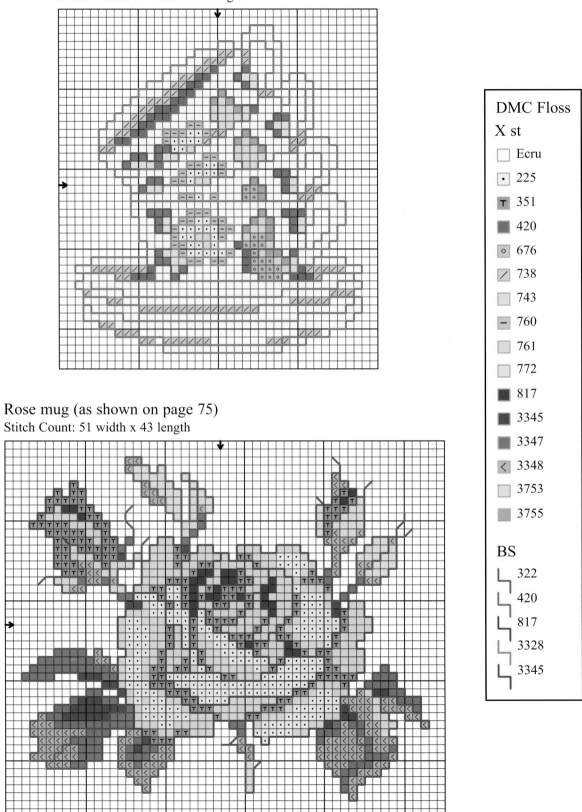

DMC Floss
X st

☐	Ecru
·	225
T	351
■	420
o	676
╱	738
☐	743
–	760
☐	761
☐	772
■	817
■	3345
■	3347
<	3348
☐	3753
■	3755

BS

⌐	322
⌐	420
⌐	817
⌐	3328
⌐	3345

Stitch Count: 49 width x 45 length

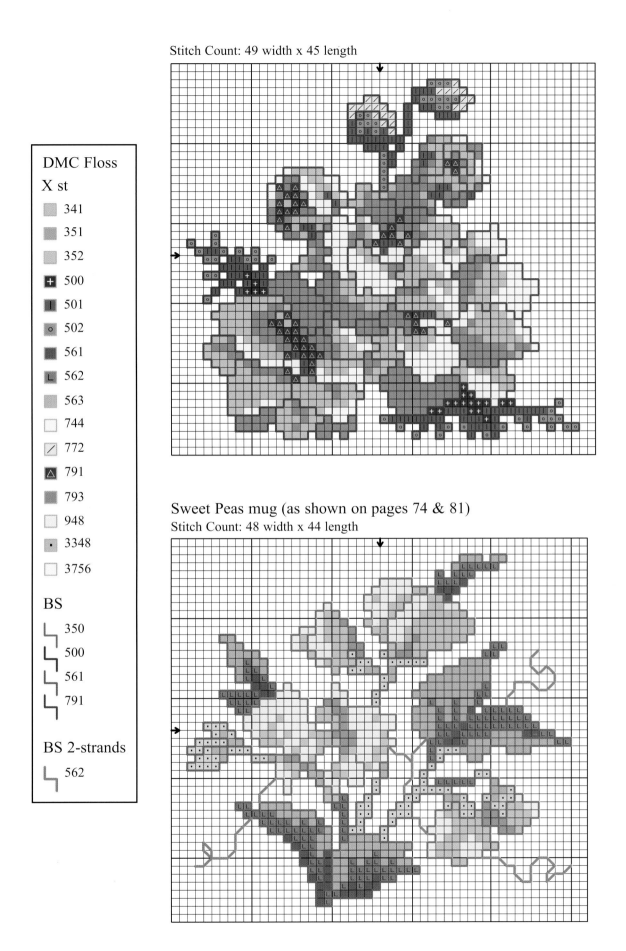

DMC Floss
X st

	341
	351
	352
+	500
I	501
o	502
	561
L	562
	563
	744
/	772
△	791
	793
	948
·	3348
	3756

BS

⌐	350
⌐	500
⌐	561
⌐	791

BS 2-strands

⌐	562

Sweet Peas mug (as shown on pages 74 & 81)
Stitch Count: 48 width x 44 length

Designs for Small
Acessories

small magnet
Stitch Count: 25 width x 25 length

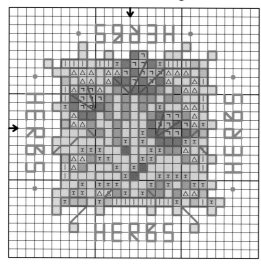

Radishes small magnet (as shown on page 87)
Stitch Count: 24 width x 25 length

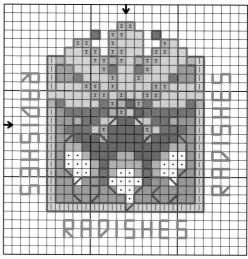

small magnet
Stitch Count: 24 width x 24 length

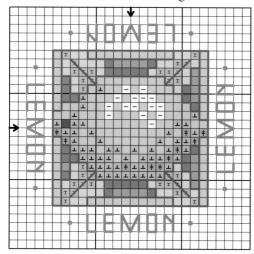

small magnet
Stitch Count: 24 width x 26 length

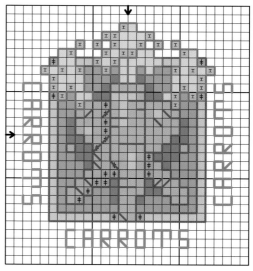

small magnet
Stitch Count: 24 width x 24 length

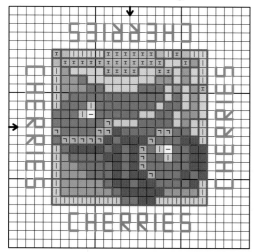

Watermelon small magnet (as shown on page 87)
Stitch Count: 24 width x 25 length

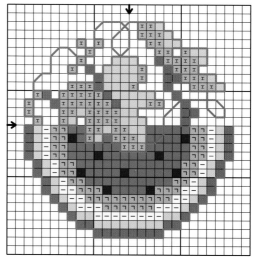

Queen keychain (as shown on page 87)
Stitch Count: 23 width x 25 length

King keychain (as shown on page 87)
Stitch Count: 22 width x 25 length

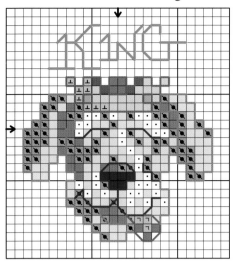

Bunny pencil topper (as shown on page 95)
Stitch Count: 25 width x 24 length

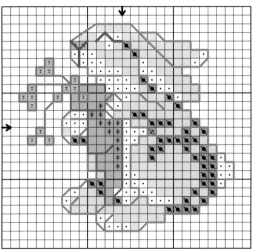

Mouse small magnet (as shown on page 86)
Stitch Count: 24 width x 25 length

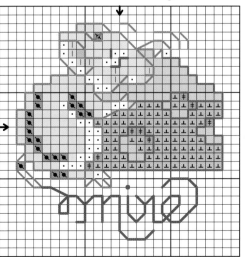

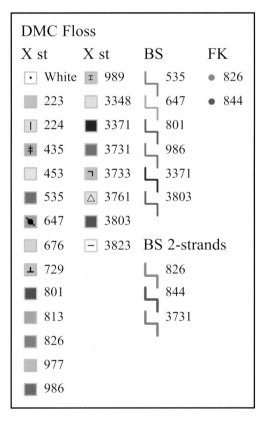

DMC Floss

X st		X st		BS		FK	
·	White	I	989		535	●	826
	223		3348		647	●	844
I	224		3371		801		
‡	435		3731		986		
	453	⌐	3733		3371		
	535	△	3761		3803		
	647		3803				
	676	−	3823	BS 2-strands			
⊥	729				826		
	801				844		
	813				3731		
	826						
	977						
	986						

small magnet
Stitch Count: 23 width x 25 length

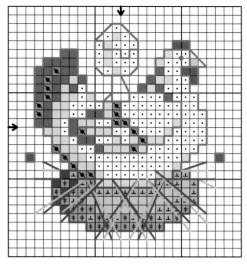

small magnet
Stitch Count: 22 width x 24 length

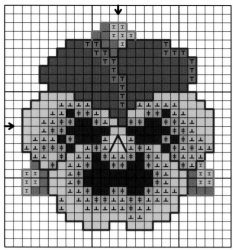

Bird keychain (as shown on page 87)
Stitch Count: 26 width x 26 length

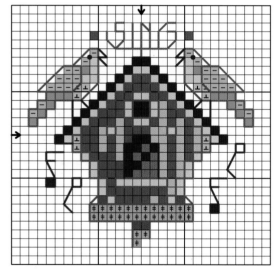

small magnet
Stitch Count: 25 width x 24 length

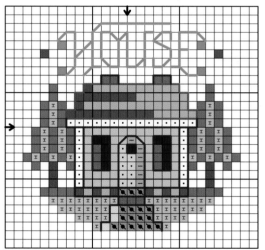

small magnet
Stitch Count: 26 width x 24 length

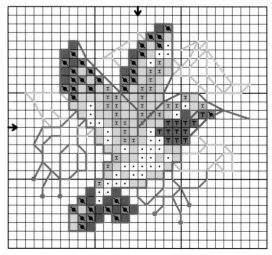

Beehive pencil topper (as shown on page 95)
Stitch Count: 26 width x 26 length

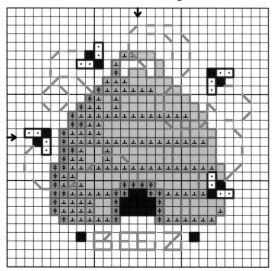

small magnet
Stitch Count: 27 width x 25 length

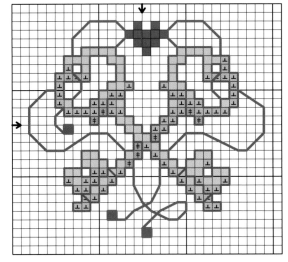

Sun keychain (as shown on page 86)
Stitch Count: 27 width x 26 length

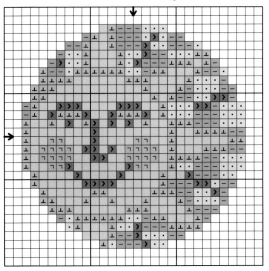

small magnet
Stitch Count: 26 width x 26 length

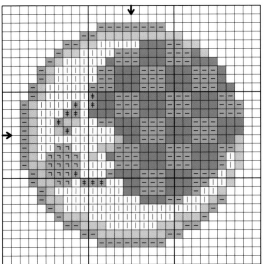

small magnet
Stitch Count: 27 width x 27 length

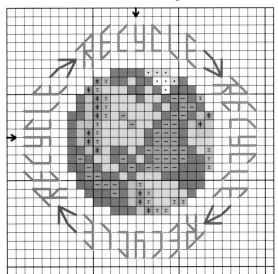

DMC Floss

X st		X st		BS		BS 2-strands	
·	White		826	⌐	434	⌐	304
	223		986	⌐	435	⌐	826
	304	I	989	⌐	535		
❯	434		3348	⌐	729	**FK**	
‡	435	■	3371	⌐	801	●	535
	453	T	3731	⌐	986	●	3371
	535	⌐	3733	⌐	989	●	3731
◖	647	·	3761	⌐	3371		
	676		3803	⌐	3731		
⊥	729	I	3823	⌐	3803		
	801						
–	813						

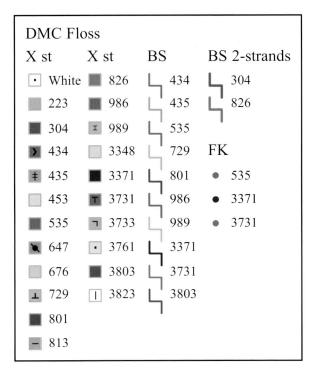

Teacher pencil topper (as shown on page 95)
Stitch Count: 24 width x 26 length

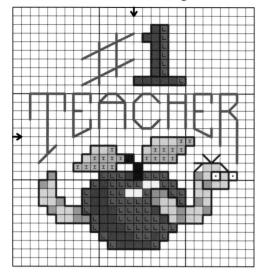

Pencil small magnet (as shown on page 87)
Stitch Count: 27 width x 21 length

Water Me pencil topper (as shown on page 95)
Stitch Count: 27 width x 25 length

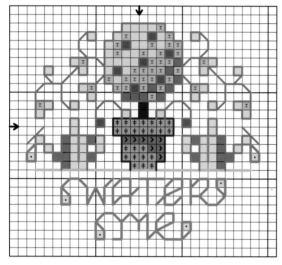

small magnet
Stitch Count: 27 width x 26 length

Grocery List small magnet (as shown on page 87)
Stitch Count: 26 width x 25 length

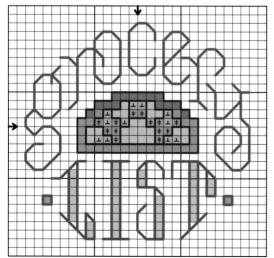

small magnet
Stitch Count: 24 width x 24 length

small magnet
Stitch Count: 26 width x 24 length

1st Place small magnet
(as shown on page 87)
Stitch Count: 20 width x 23 length

small magnet
Stitch Count: 24 width x 24 length

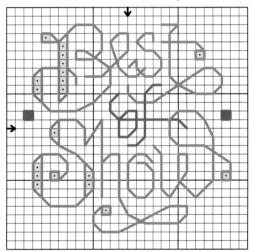

small magnet
Stitch Count: 30 width x 27 length

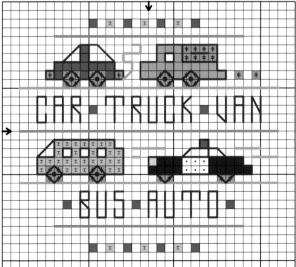

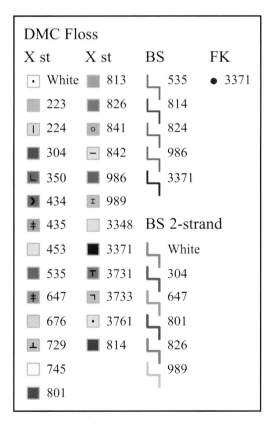

DMC Floss			
X st	X st	BS	FK
· White	813	└ 535	● 3371
223	826	└ 814	
I 224	o 841	└ 824	
304	− 842	└ 986	
L 350	986	└ 3371	
⟩ 434	I 989		
‡ 435	3348	BS 2-strand	
453	3371	└ White	
535	T 3731	└ 304	
‡ 647	¬ 3733	└ 647	
676	· 3761	└ 801	
⊥ 729	814	└ 826	
745		└ 989	
801			

small magnet
Stitch Count: 24 width x 22 length

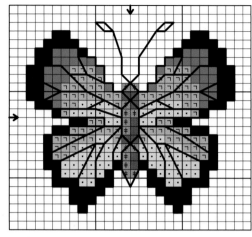

magnet
Stitch Count: 30 width x 22 length

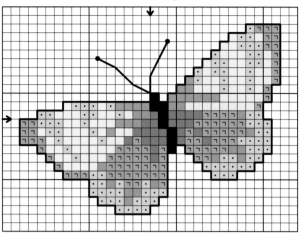

small magnet
Stitch Count: 24 width x 24 length

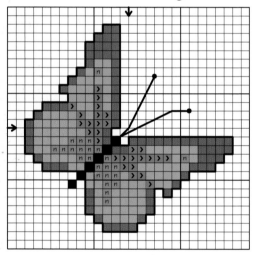

DMC Floss			
X st		**X st**	
o	309		3705
■	310	/	3706
	400	⊓	3766
	598		3799
‡	647	›	3810
−	676	·	3811
	744	n	3826
	783		
	806	**BS**	
	815	⌐	310
I	899		
T	958	**FK**	
I	959	•	310

small magnet
Stitch Count: 16 width x 17 length

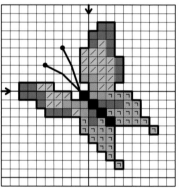

small magnet
Stitch Count: 20 width x 20 length

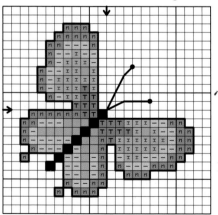

small magnet
Stitch Count: 13 width x 13 length

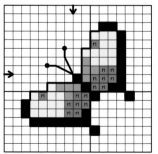

small magnet
Stitch Count: 13 width x 15 length

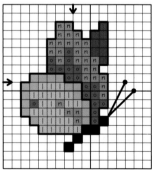

magnet
Stitch Count: 25 width x 29 length

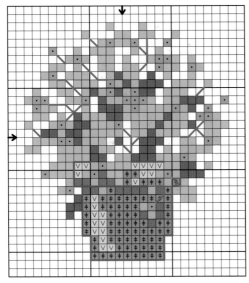

magnet
Stitch Count: 26 width x 29 length

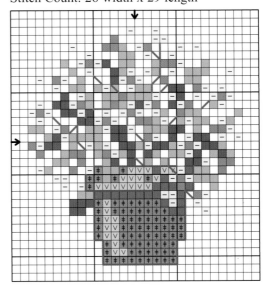

magnet
Stitch Count: 28 width x 23 length

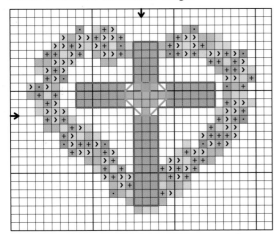

small magnet
Stitch Count: 27 width x 24 length

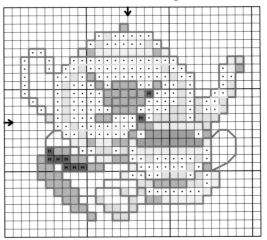

Pansy luggage tag (as shown on page 95)
Stitch Count: 29 width x 29 length

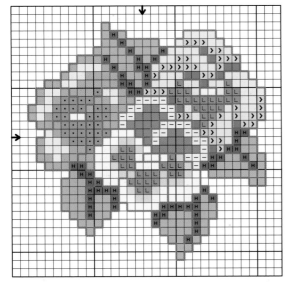

Humming Bird magnet (as shown on page 86)
Stitch Count: 28 width x 30 length

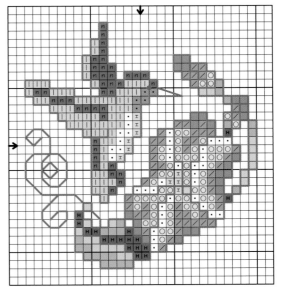

Flower Basket key ring (as shown on page 86)
Stitch Count: 26 width x 34 length

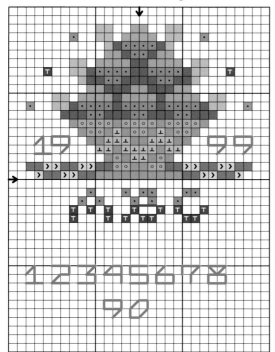

luggage tag
Stitch Count: 24 width x 28 length

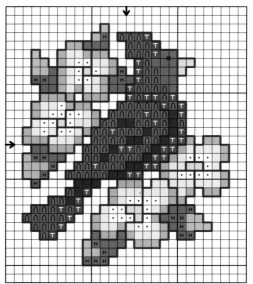

magnet
Stitch Count: 28 width x 27 length

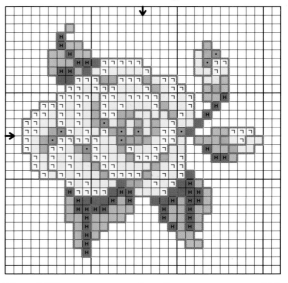

DMC Floss

X st		X st		BS	
·	White	■	826		535
■	209	■	902		801
−	211	V	950		986
∩	321		963		3371
L	340	■	986		3731
■	435	H	987		3822
■	535	■	989		
I	564	n	992	**BS 2-strands**	
■	632	□	3078		816
⊥	676	·	3731		826
o	729	■	3733		
	772	I	3743	**FK**	
	775	O	3747	●	535
■	793	❭	3761	●	3371
/	794	‡	3772		
+	807	■	3803		
T	816		3822		
ꓶ	819				

Floral Heart magnet (as shown on page 87)
Stitch Count: 27 width x 25 length

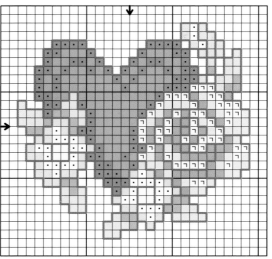

small magnet
Stitch Count: 24 width x 24 length

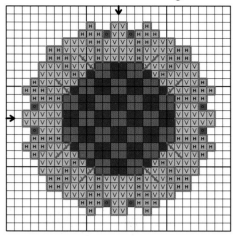

magnet
Stitch Count: 26 width x 27 length

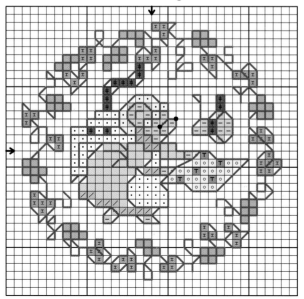

Chilies magnet (as shown on page 87)
Stitch Count: 29 width x 30 length

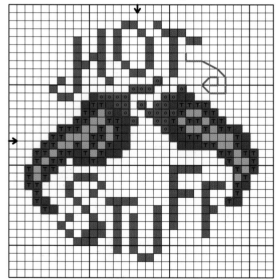

magnet
Stitch Count: 25 width x 29 length

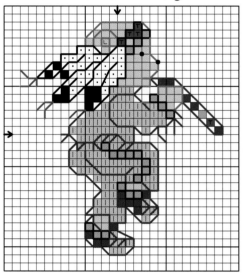

Chocolates magnet (as shown on page 86)
Stitch Count: 30 width x 30 length

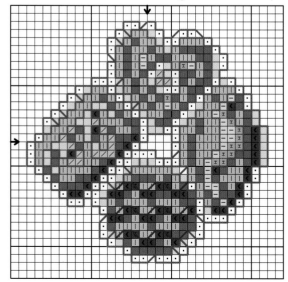

Mrs. Mouse magnet (as shown on page 86)
Stitch Count: 32 width x 32 length

Noah's Ark luggage tag (as shown on page 95)
Stitch Count: 30 width x 30 length

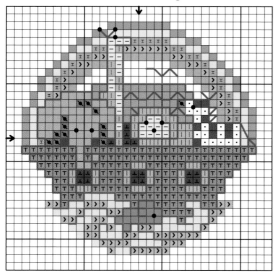

Sailboat luggage tag (as shown on page 95)
Stitch Count: 30 width x 30 length

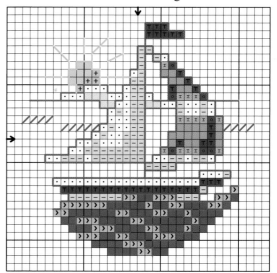

luggage tag
Stitch Count: 29 width x 29 length

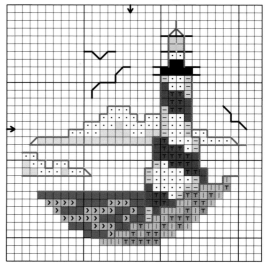

Sports luggage tag (as shown on page 95)
Stitch Count: 30 width x 30 length

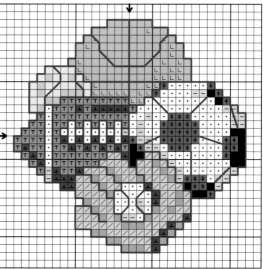

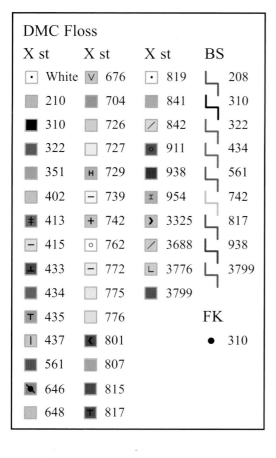

DMC Floss			
X st	X st	X st	BS
· White	V 676	· 819	208
210	704	841	310
310	726	/ 842	322
322	727	o 911	434
351	H 729	938	561
402	− 739	I 954	742
‡ 413	+ 742	> 3325	817
− 415	o 762	/ 3688	938
⊥ 433	− 772	L 3776	3799
434	775	3799	
T 435	776		FK
I 437	◄ 801		● 310
561	807		
◣ 646	815		
648	T 817		

Designs for Bookmarks

Best Friends grow together with love!

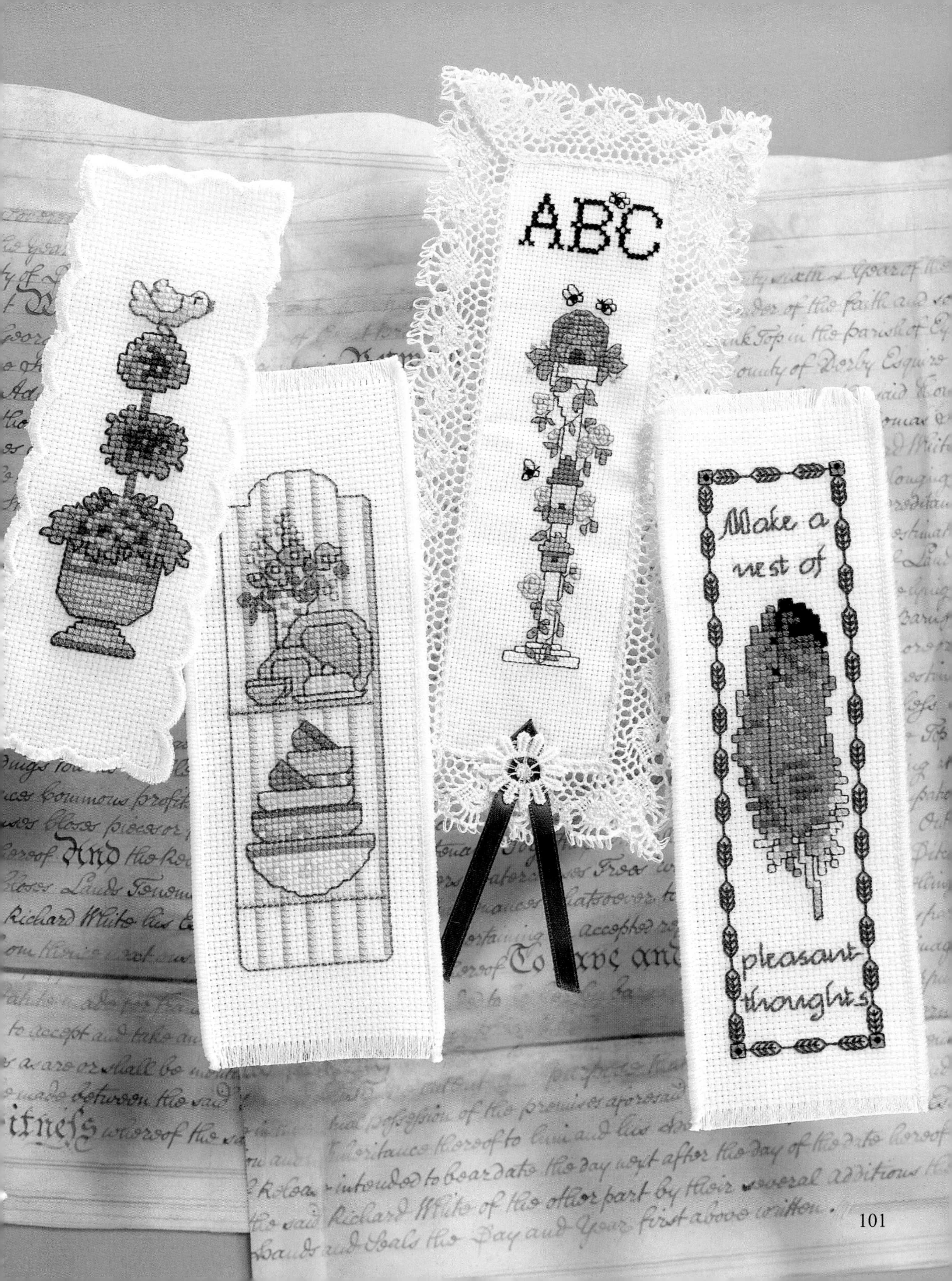
ABC
Make a nest of
pleasant thoughts

Feather bookmark (as shown on page 101)
Stitch Count: 24 width x 93 length

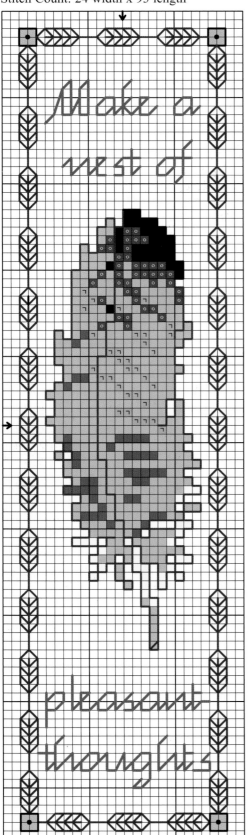

Fishing bookmark (as shown on page 100)
Stitch Count: 26 width x 96 length

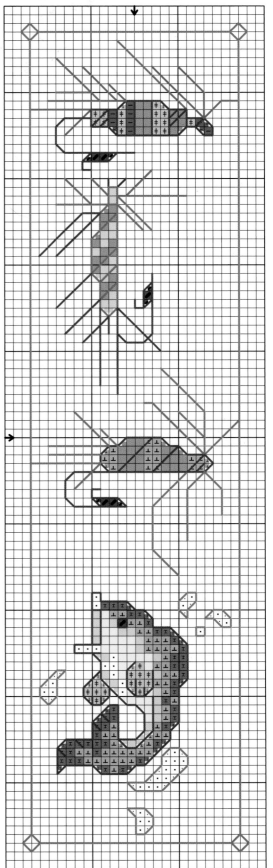

Stitch Count: 27 width x 65 length   Stitch Count: 30 width x 69 length

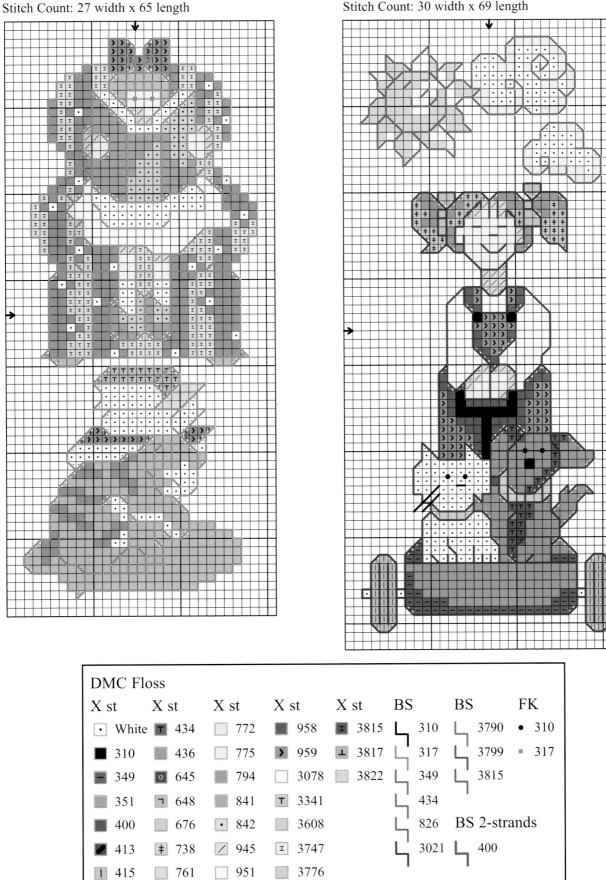

DMC Floss

	X st		X st		X st		X st		X st	BS		BS		FK	
·	White	T	434		772	■	958	I	3815	⌐	310	⌐	3790	●	310
■	310		436		775	›	959	⊥	3817	⌐	317	⌐	3799	●	317
─	349	o	645		794		3078		3822	⌐	349	⌐	3815		
	351	⌐	648		841	T	3341			⌐	434				
■	400		676	·	842		3608			⌐	826	BS 2-strands			
◢	413	‡	738	/	945	I	3747			⌐	3021	⌐	400		
I	415		761		951		3776								

103

Stitch Count: 26 width x 96 length

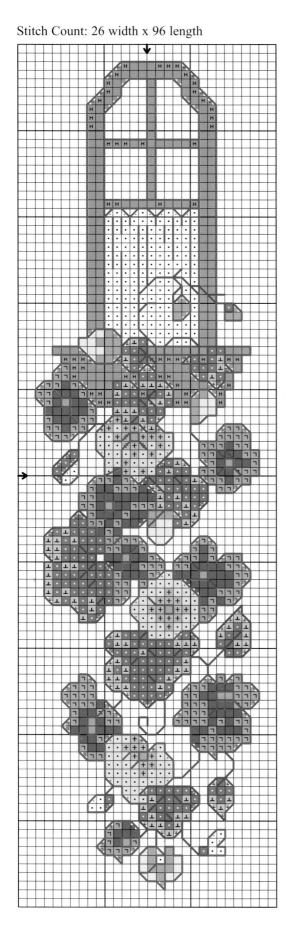

Birdhouse bookmark (as shown on page 101)
Stitch Count: 28 width x 98 length

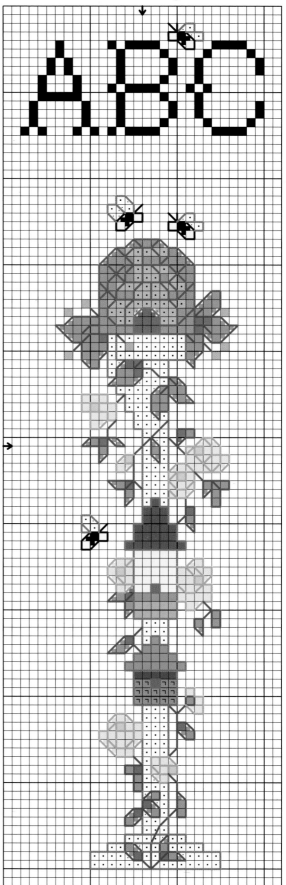

Topiary bookmark (as shown on page 101)
Stitch Count: 24 width x 61 length

Stitch Count: 17 width x 41 length

**Butterfly bookmark
(as shown on page 109)**
Stitch Count: 21 width x 80 length

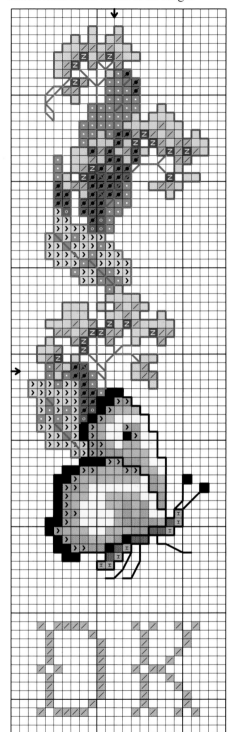

DMC Floss

X st		X st		X st		X st		BS		BS 2-strands	
·	White	·	437	L	746	n	3325	⌐	310	⌐	3348
	210		598	T	747		3326	⌐	319		
■	310	·	605	⊥	772	·	3347	⌐	335		
o	319		632		775	›	3348	⌐	413		
	334	‡	699	H	807	+	3608	⌐	699		
╱	335		702	Z	816	⊥	3778	⌐	816		
	350		704		818		38268	⌐	915		
⌐	352	·	718	I	841			⌐	975		
	413		722		915			⌐	986		
›	414		725		986						
	435	☐	745	◕	987						

Stitch Count: 27 width x 90 length

Stitch Count: 28 width x 89 length

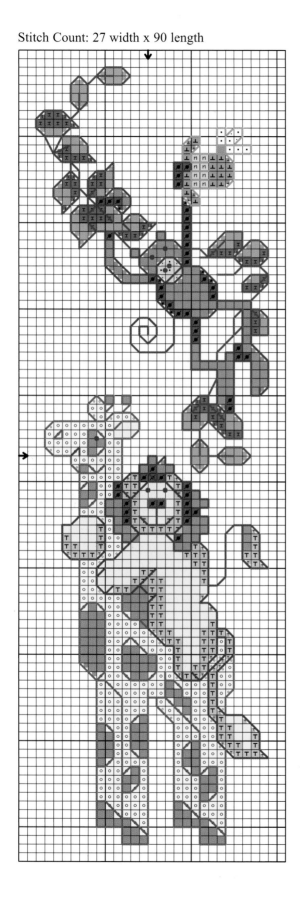

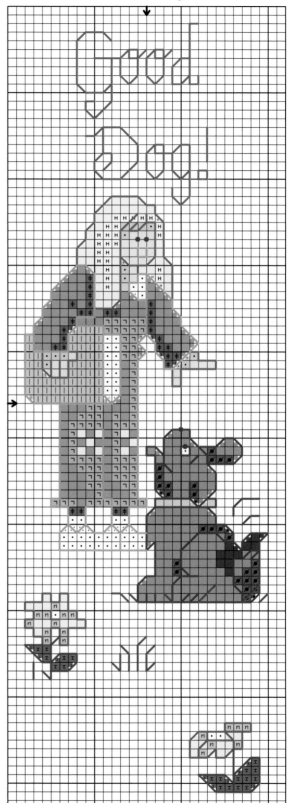

Stitch Count: 28 width x 56 length

Stitch Count: 26 width x 61 length

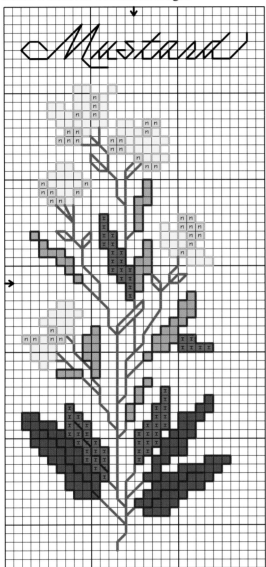

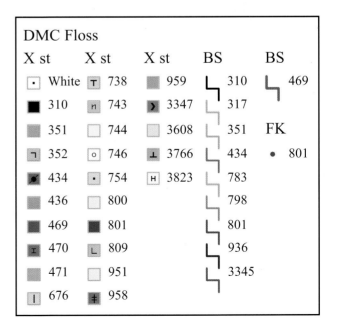

DMC Floss				
X st	X st	X st	BS	BS
· White	T 738	▨ 959	⌐ 310	⌐ 469
■ 310	n 743	▶ 3347	⌐ 317	
▨ 351	☐ 744	▨ 3608	⌐ 351	FK
⌐ 352	o 746	⊥ 3766	⌐ 434	• 801
◕ 434	· 754	H 3823	⌐ 783	
▨ 436	☐ 800		⌐ 798	
▨ 469	■ 801		⌐ 801	
I 470	L 809		⌐ 936	
▨ 471	☐ 951		⌐ 3345	
I 676	‡ 958			

107

Stitch Count: 26 width x 55 length

Stitch Count: 27 width x 57 length

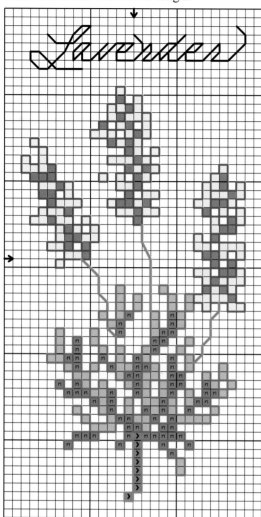

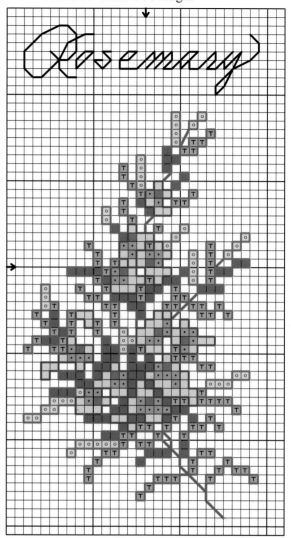

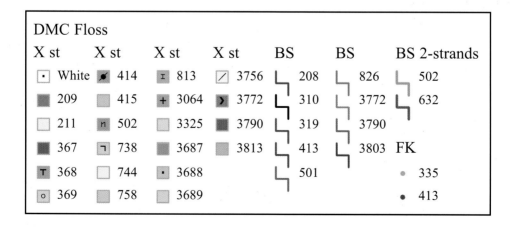

DMC Floss

X st		X st		X st		X st		BS	BS	BS 2-strands
·	White	414	I	813	/	3756		208	826	502
	209		415	+	3064		3772	310	3772	632
	211	n	502		3325		3790	319	3790	
	367	7	738		3687		3813	413	3803	FK
T	368		744	·	3688			501		· 335
o	369		758		3689					· 413

108

Stitch Count: 28 width x 95 length

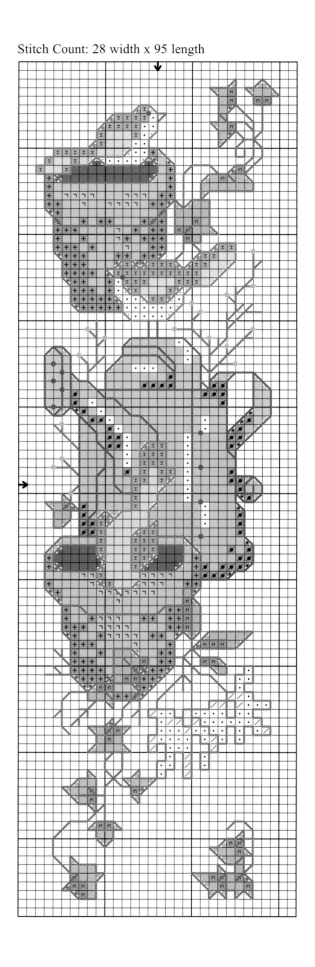

Dove & Heart bookmark (as shown on page 109)
Stitch Count: 28 width x 73 length

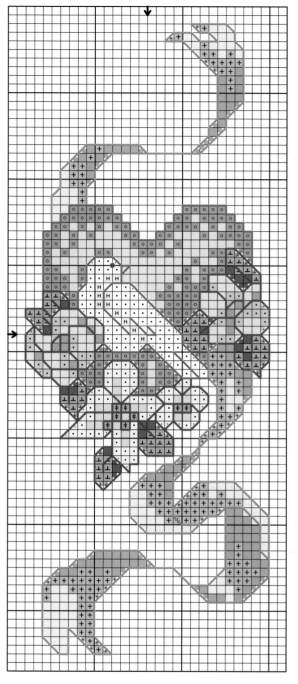

Baker's Rack bookmark
(as shown on page 101)
Stitch Count: 24 width x 79 length

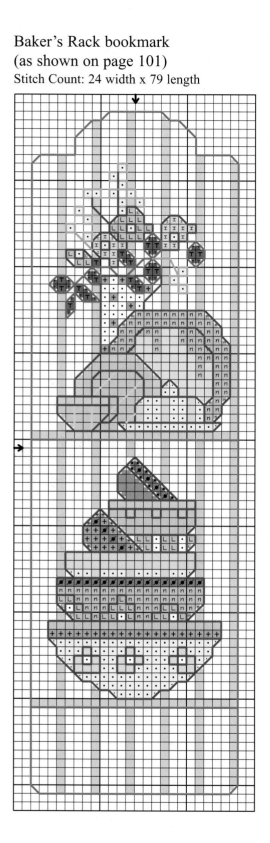

DMC Floss					
X st	X st	X st	X st	BS	FK
· White	‡ 722	818	⊥ 3817	208	• 413
209	744	964	· 3823	413	
+ 210	772	· 3326		562	
211	⚫ 793	L 3341		826	
335	794	n 3753		841	
T 562	800	H 3756		964	
I 605	o 813	3815			

Best Friends bookmark
(as shown on page 100)
Stitch Count: 25 width x 89 length

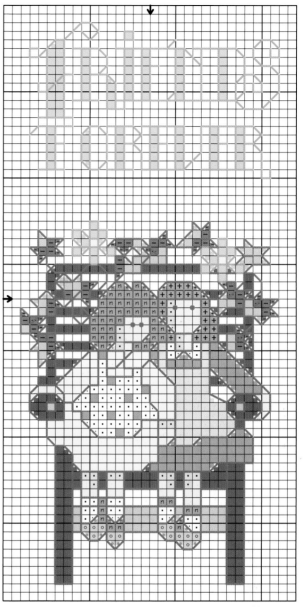

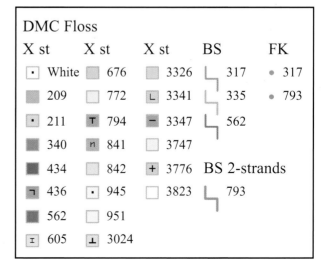

DMC Floss				
X st	X st	X st	BS	FK
· White	676	3326	⌐ 317	• 317
209	772	L 3341	⌐ 335	• 793
· 211	T 794	— 3347	⌐ 562	
340	n 841	3747		
434	842	+ 3776	BS 2-strands	
⌐ 436	· 945	3823	⌐ 793	
562	951			
I 605	⊥ 3024			

111

Stitch Count: 28 width x 80 length

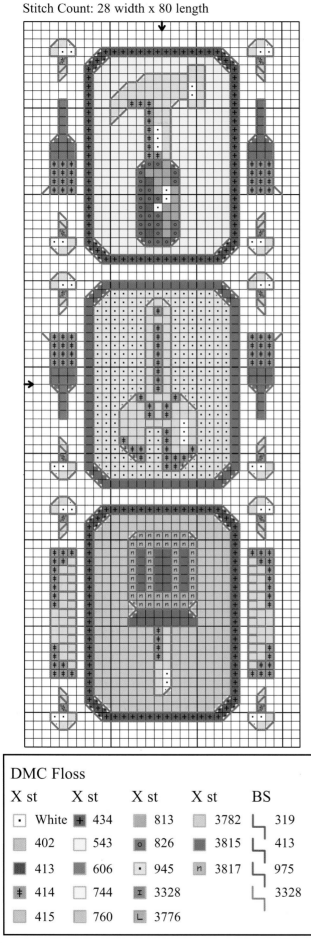

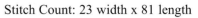

Stitch Count: 23 width x 81 length

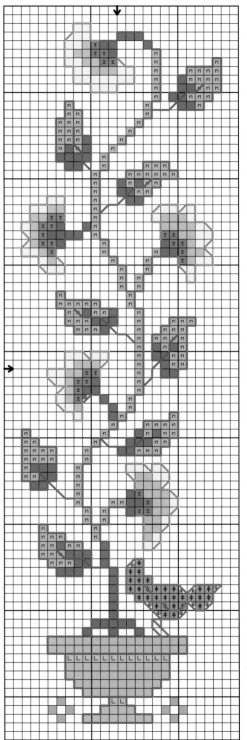

DMC Floss				
X st	X st	X st	X st	BS
· White	+ 434	813	3782	⌐ 319
402	543	o 826	3815	⌐ 413
413	606	· 945	n 3817	⌐ 975
+ 414	744	I 3328		⌐ 3328
415	760	L 3776		

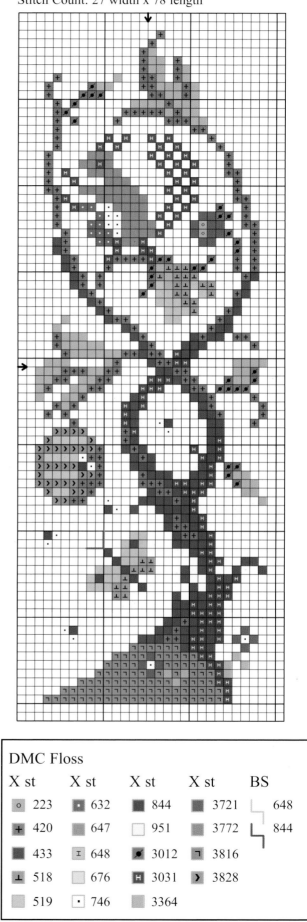

Birds bookmark (as shown on page 100)
Stitch Count: 27 width x 79 length

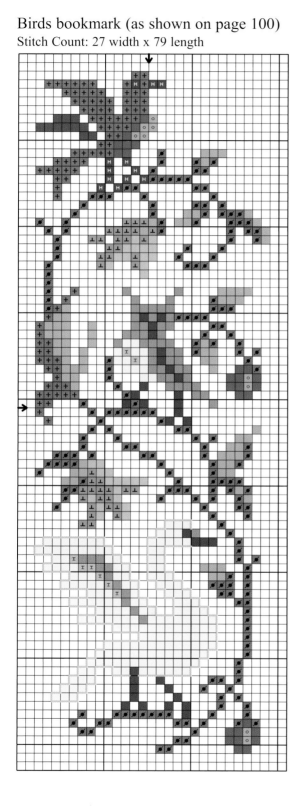

DMC Floss				
X st	X st	X st	X st	BS
o 223	▪ 632	■ 844	■ 3721	⌐ 648
+ 420	647	□ 951	3772	└ 844
■ 433	ɪ 648	✿ 3012	⌐ 3816	
⊥ 518	676	н 3031	❯ 3828	
519	• 746	3364		

113

Designs for Christmas

Angel oval ornament (as shown on page 114)
Stitch Count: 26 width x 40 length

Stitch Count: 20 width x 20 length

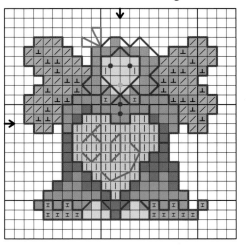

Stitch Count: 22 width x 21 length

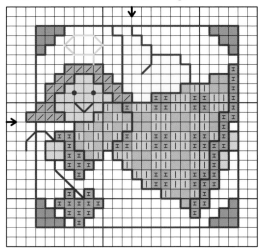

Stitch Count: 28 width x 38 length

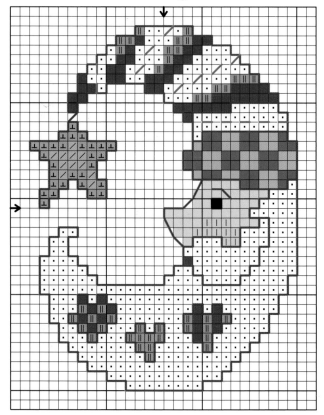

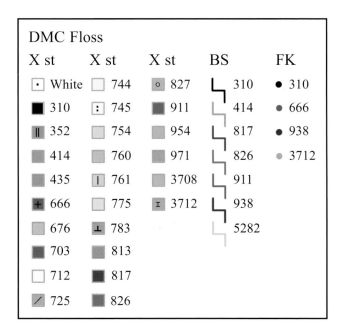

DMC Floss

	X st		X st		X st	BS	FK
·	White	☐	744	○	827	310	● 310
■	310	:	745	■	911	414	● 666
‖	352		754		954	817	● 938
	414		760		971	826	● 3712
	435	‖	761		3708	911	
+	666		775	I	3712	938	
	676	⊥	783			5282	
	703		813				
☐	712		817				
/	725		826				

NOEL octagonal ornament
(as shown on page 114)
Stitch Count: 21 width x 21 length

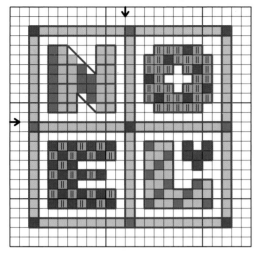

Santa Sign oval ornament
(as shown on page 115)
Stitch Count: 23 width x 41 length

Snowman oval ornament (as shown on page 115)
Stitch Count: 28 width x 37 length

Stitch Count: 28 width x 39 length

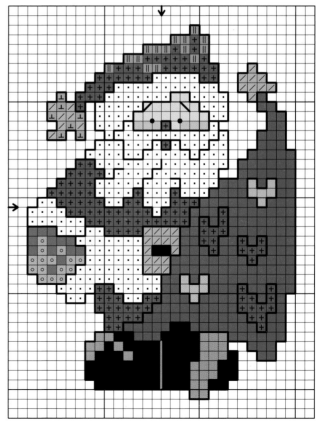

Angel stocking ornament (as shown on page 121)
Stitch Count: 38 width x 51 length

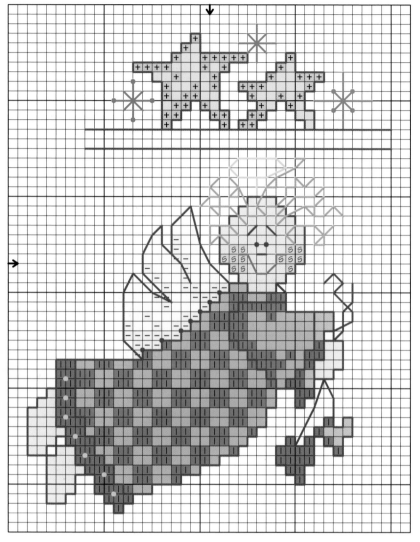

Stitch Count: 21 width x 21 length

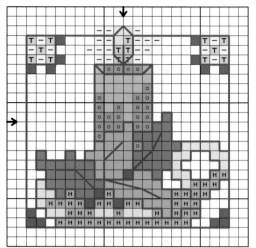

Stitch Count: 21 width x 21 length

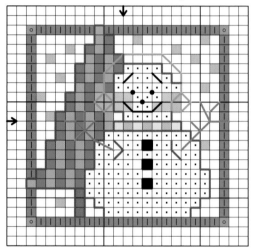

Stitch Count: 26 width x 26 length

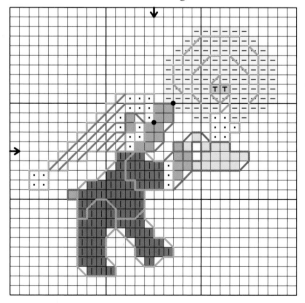

Hearts & Stars octagonal ornament (as shown on page 115)
Stitch Count: 22 width x 21 length

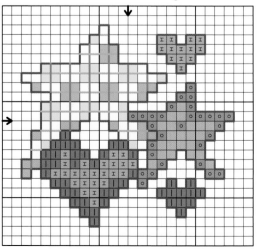

Santa snowflake ornament
(as shown on page 115)
Stitch Count: 19 width x 21 length

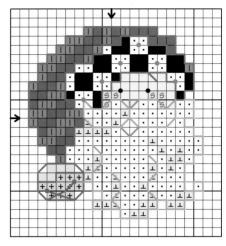

Stitch Count: 16 width x 22 length

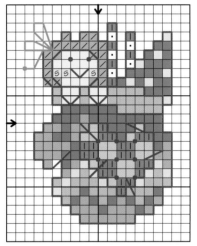

Santa Claus snowflake ornament
(as shown on page 121)
Stitch Count: 19 width x 27 length

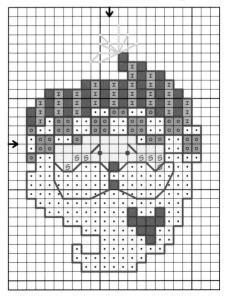

Teddy Bear stocking ornament (as shown on page 121)
Stitch Count: 41 width x 52 length

DMC Floss				
X st	X st	X st	BS	FK
· White	o 798	+ 3820	310	● 310
■ 310	799	3823	349	● 349
I 349	I 806	3827	351	● 806
I 351	817		400	● 817
400	911		414	● 911
H 414	913		742	● 938
415	938		798	● 3799
L 739	948		911	● 3820
740	I 963		938	
T 742	/ 976		976	
743	3708		3799	
− 744	⊥ 3753		5282	
S 761	3766			

Penguin stocking ornament (as shown on page 121)
Stitch Count: 42 width x 51 length

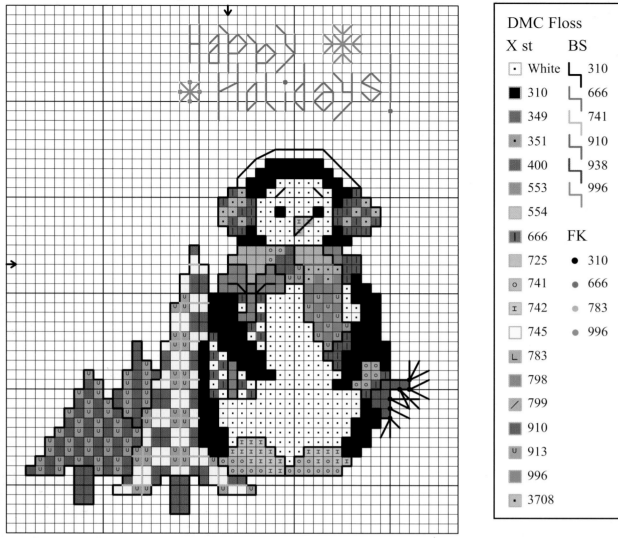

DMC Floss

X st		BS	
·	White	⌐	310
■	310	⌐	666
■	349	⌐	741
·	351	⌐	910
■	400	⌐	938
■	553	⌐	996
	554		
I	666		FK
	725	●	310
o	741	●	666
I	742	●	783
	745	●	996
L	783		
	798		
/	799		
	910		
U	913		
	996		
·	3708		

Heart octagonal ornament (as shown on page 114)
Stitch Count: 27 width x 26 length

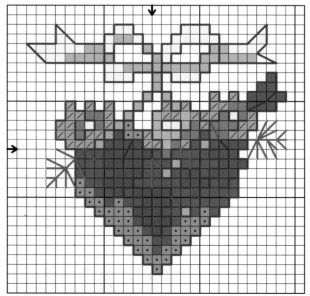

Stitch Count: 29 width x 25 length

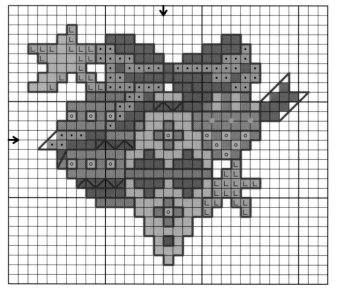

stocking ornament
Stitch Count: 48 width x 54 length

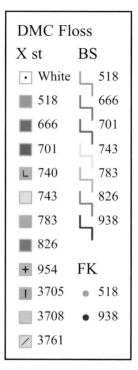

DMC Floss

X st		BS	
·	White	⌐	518
▨	518	⌐	666
■	666	⌐	701
■	701	⌐	743
L	740	⌐	783
▨	743	⌐	826
▨	783	⌐	938
■	826		
+	954	**FK**	
I	3705	●	518
▨	3708	●	938
╱	3761		

Hearts, Stars & Candy heart ornament
(as shown on page 115)
Stitch Count: 29 width x 27 length

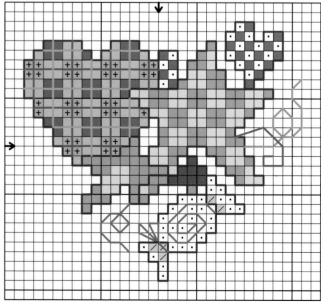

Stitch Count: 27 width x 26 length

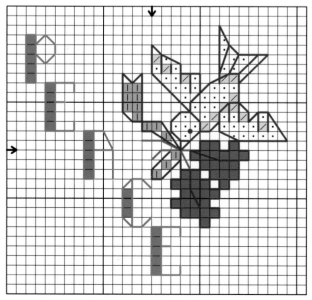

122

stocking ornament
Stitch Count: 40 width x 53 length

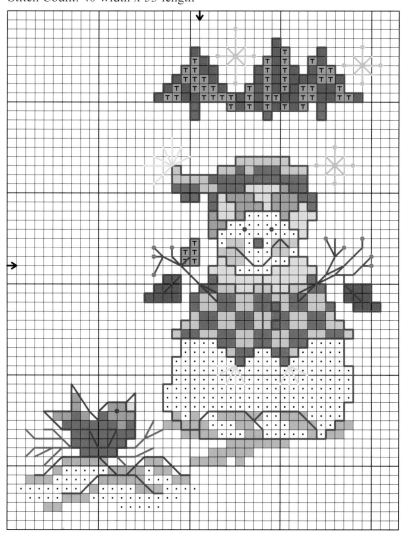

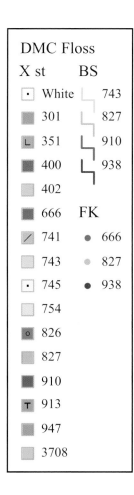

DMC Floss

X st		BS	
·	White		743
■	301		827
L	351		910
■	400		938
	402		
■	666	FK	
/	741	●	666
	743	●	827
·	745	●	938
	754		
o	826		
	827		
	910		
T	913		
	947		
	3708		

Candles heart ornament
(as shown on page 114)
Stitch Count: 24 width x 27 length

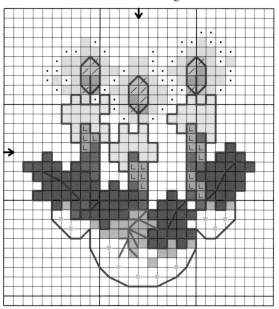

Stitch Count: 32 width x 29 length

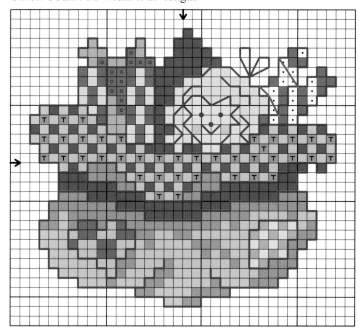

123

stocking ornament
Stitch Count: 41 width x 49 length

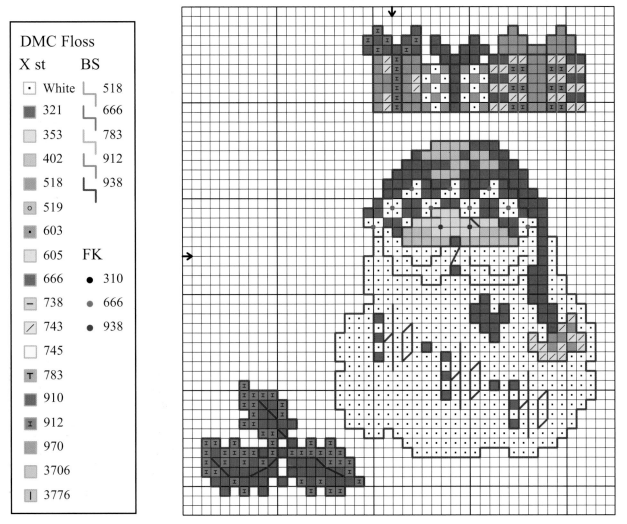

DMC Floss

X st		BS	
·	White	└	518
■	321	└	666
▨	353	└	783
▦	402	└	912
▩	518	└	938
o	519		
⦁	603		
▢	605	**FK**	
■	666	●	310
−	738	●	666
╱	743	●	938
▢	745		
T	783		
■	910		
I	912		
▨	970		
▧	3706		
I	3776		

Stitch Count: 24 width x 21 length

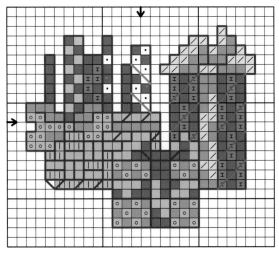

Angel octagonal ornament (as shown on page 115)
Stitch Count: 27 width x 23 length

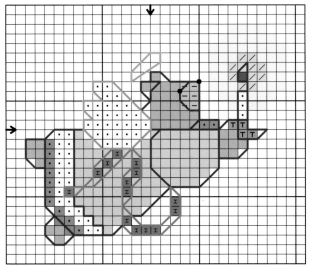

Snowman snowflake ornament
(as shown on page 114)
Stitch Count: 21 width x 22 length

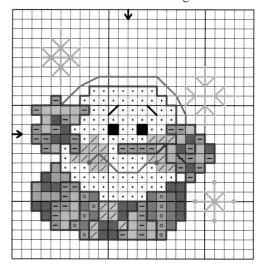

Stitch Count: 22 width x 22 length

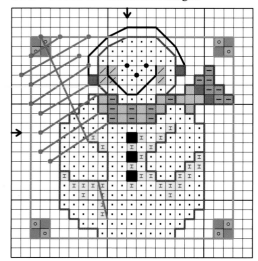

Stitch Count: 23 width x 22 length

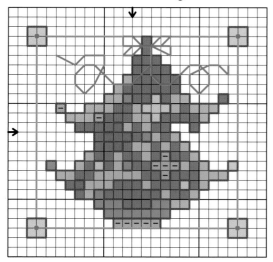

Wreath snowflake ornament
(as shown on page 115)
Stitch Count: 21 width x 23 length

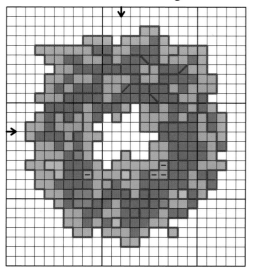

Stitch Count: 20 width x 21 length

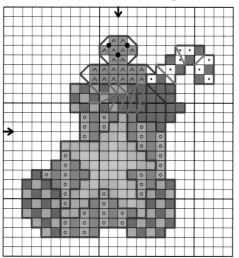

DMC Floss

X st		X st		BS		FK	
·	White	■	826		310	●	310
■	310	■	910		400	●	666
■	666		913		666	●	813
	725	∧	922		813		
I	775	—	947		826		
	783		3705		910		
o	813	/	3706		938		

Alphabets

Mug Alphabet

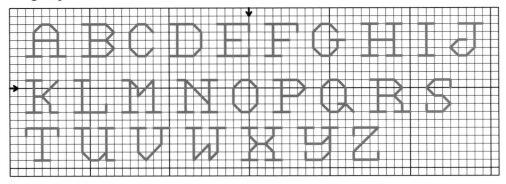

Bookmark Alphabet

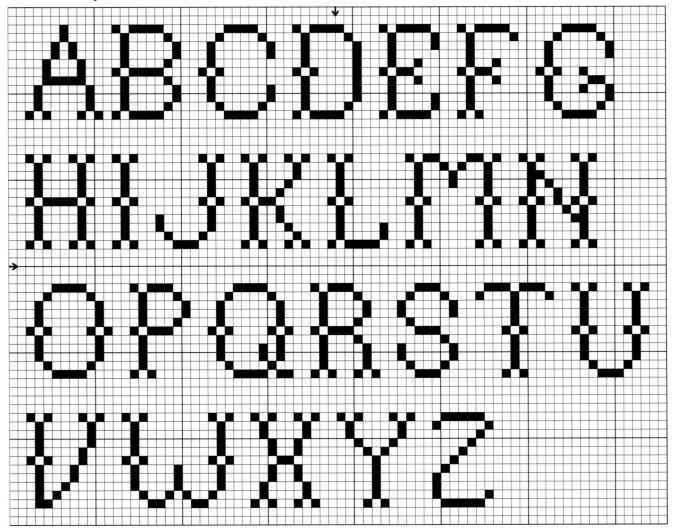

Metric Equivalency Chart

mm-millimetres   cm-centimetres
inches to millimetres and centimetres

inches	mm	cm	inches	cm	inches	cm
⅛	3	0.3	9	22.9	30	76.2
¼	6	0.6	10	25.4	31	78.7
⅜	10	1.0	11	27.9	32	81.3
½	13	1.3	12	30.5	33	83.8
⅝	16	1.6	13	33.0	34	86.4
¾	19	1.9	14	35.6	35	88.9
⅞	22	2.2	15	38.1	36	91.4
1	25	2.5	16	40.6	37	94.0
1¼	32	3.2	17	43.2	38	96.5
1½	38	3.8	18	45.7	39	99.1
1¾	44	4.4	19	48.3	40	101.6
2	51	5.1	20	50.8	41	104.1
2½	64	6.4	21	53.3	42	106.7
3	76	7.6	22	55.9	43	109.2
3½	89	8.9	23	58.4	44	111.8
4	102	10.2	24	61.0	45	114.3
4½	114	11.4	25	63.5	46	116.8
5	127	12.7	26	66.0	47	119.4
6	152	15.2	27	68.6	48	121.9
7	178	17.8	28	71.1	49	124.5
8	203	20.3	29	73.7	50	127.0

yards to metres

yards	metres	yards	metres	yards	metres	yards	metres	yards	metres
⅛	0.11	2⅛	1.94	4⅛	3.77	6⅛	5.60	8⅛	7.43
¼	0.23	2¼	2.06	4¼	3.89	6¼	5.72	8¼	7.54
⅜	0.34	2⅜	2.17	4⅜	4.00	6⅜	5.83	8⅜	7.66
½	0.46	2½	2.29	4½	4.11	6½	5.94	8½	7.77
⅝	0.57	2⅝	2.40	4⅝	4.23	6⅝	6.06	8⅝	7.89
¾	0.69	2¾	2.51	4¾	4.34	6¾	6.17	8¾	8.00
⅞	0.80	2⅞	2.63	4⅞	4.46	6⅞	6.29	8⅞	8.12
1	0.91	3	2.74	5	4.57	7	6.40	9	8.23
1⅛	1.03	3⅛	2.86	5⅛	4.69	7⅛	6.52	9⅛	8.34
1¼	1.14	3¼	2.97	5¼	4.80	7¼	6.63	9¼	8.46
1⅜	1.26	3⅜	3.09	5⅜	4.91	7⅜	6.74	9⅜	8.57
1½	1.37	3½	3.20	5½	5.03	7½	6.86	9½	8.69
1⅝	1.49	3⅝	3.31	5⅝	5.14	7⅝	6.97	9⅝	8.80
1¾	1.60	3¾	3.43	5¾	5.26	7¾	7.09	9¾	8.92
1⅞	1.71	3⅞	3.54	5⅞	5.37	7⅞	7.20	9⅞	9.03
2	1.83	4	3.66	6	5.49	8	7.32	10	9.14

Index